HOT TIPS FOR SUCCESS ON
WHO WANTS TO BE A MILLIONAIRE?

● **Hot Tip!** When calling in to get picked for the show: Many of the show's phone-based questions are related to **holidays and geography**. Be sure to have a calendar, a list of national holidays, and two small, but legible maps (one of the world, one of the U.S.) on hand.

● **Hot Tip!** Once you've gotten picked for the show, remember to **dress warmly** (the studio is very cold), **know the format** of your keyboard in the qualifying round (it's A B C D OK), and **use your lifelines carefully** (for instance, if you have a pop-culture question you're unsure of, choose the "Ask the Audience" option—that's a subject they're almost always right about).

● **Hot Tip!** <u>Relax</u>. Nothing will jeopardize your chances of winning more than feeling nervous and acting impulsively. Think out your answers carefully and take all the time you need. Sitting across from Regis Philbin, who shows his warmth and humanity with his sense of humor and by frequently mispronouncing words, should help a lot.

FIND OUT MORE HINTS
FOR WINNING BIG INSIDE

SO YOU'D LIKE TO WIN A MILLION

ST. MARTIN'S PAPERBACKS TITLES
BY ELINA AND LEAH FURMAN

Enrique Iglesias

James Van Der Beek

Lyte Funkie Ones

SO YOU'D LIKE TO WIN A MILLION

FACTS, TRIVIA, AND HINTS ON GAME SHOW SUCCESS

ELINA & LEAH FURMAN

St. Martin's Paperbacks

SO YOU'D LIKE TO WIN A MILLION: FACTS, TRIVIA, AND HINTS ON GAME SHOW SUCCESS

ISBN: 0-312-97635-6

Printed in the United States of America

St. Martin's Paperbacks edition / February 2000

10 9 8 7 6 5 4 3 2 1

FOR MOM

ACKNOWLEDGMENTS

We'd like to thank Joe Veltre for thinking of us for this project, and our agent, Giles Anderson, for being there every step of the way. We'd also like to thank John Nikkah for helping us fine-tune our sports trivia, and our mother, Mira, whose help and support we could never do without.

TABLE OF CONTENTS

PART I

THE SHOWS

THE GREATEST SHOWS ON EARTH

A million dollars. We've heard those three little words often enough, but what do they really mean? It's just a figure, after all. Nothing but a nice round sum, petty cash to the likes of Bill Gates, a punchline in the *Austin Powers* movies, a poor lottery jackpot to the Superball fanatics, a week's work to Julia Roberts and the rest of Hollywood's $20 million club. But then again, imagine seeing all those zeroes on your bank statement . . . $1,000,000.00. Talk about regaining your sense of perspective.

People have been known to kill for far less. Luckily, you won't have to resort to any such drastic measures to make your first million. The day of the $15,000 big *Jeopardy* win and the $50,000 *Wheel of Fortune* triumph has given rise to the night of the high-stakes game shows. One hundred thousand dollars, well, that's just a bowl of small potatoes to these quiz show titans. We're talking millions here, and there's absolutely no reason why you shouldn't get in on the ground floor of the action.

So now that you're thinking big, what *would* you do with a million dollars if it was burning a hot little hole in your bank account? That seems to be the question on everyone's mind, and if you really want to win the prime-time booty (and, let's face it, who doesn't), you've got to know the answer.

While a million dollars won't buy you a townhouse in the heart of San Francisco, a deluxe penthouse in

Manhattan or a Beverly Hills manse the size of Aaron Spelling's, it should be enough to cover a three-bedroom home anywhere in the United States. If boats and cars are your passion, dream no more: a million dollars will put you at the wheel of any vehicle you shake your wallet at. Feeling fiscally responsible? Well, then a million dollars can be your retirement nest egg and your kids' college fund all wrapped up into one. Even a life of leisure can be yours for the taking, provided of course that your financial planning is sound.

The long and short of it is that becoming a millionaire can be to your advantage. But you probably already know all that. The rub is in the how?

ABC's *Who Wants to Be a Millionaire* is just one way to win the big money. With a prize ceiling of $2 million (now we're talking Manhattan penthouses), Fox's *Greed* is no slouch, either. NBC's *Twenty-One* gives you yet a third chance to score big. And if all that isn't enough, CBS has recently come up with a souped-up version of *The $64,000 Question*, and don't be surprised if the six-figure payoff puts its relatively tame name to shame (word has it that the new game will be titled *The $1,064,000 Question*).

Believe it or not, these shows are just the tip of the iceberg that is the quiz show revival. More are on the way. Even as you read, networks are scrambling to come up with additional low-cost, high-profit ratings giants whose sole purpose is to make money by giving it away.

Of course, the lump sums of liquid assets don't go to just anyone. Unless your plan is to rough it on CBS's *Survivor!* (a game which deposits sixteen contestants on a deserted island and gives a mill to the last person left standing), you need a head full of trivia and plenty of confidence to win. That's where this book comes in. We'll tell you all about the various games, the behind-the-scenes drama, the insider's secrets, and the many ways to ensure you get your fair shot at the money. More important, we'll test your knowlege and put you on the road to bagging the score of a lifetime.

But ask yourself this, how much time is a million dollars worth to you? Are you prepared to spend one hour per day for three months running? Can you make a commitment to winning and then stick to it? If your answer is yes, then don't wait another second. Let's get started.

CHAPTER ONE

WHO WANTS TO BE A MILLIONAIRE

The grand-daddy of all million dollar jackpots, the show that started the phenomenon is . . . a) *Greed* b) *Jeopardy* c) *Twenty-One* d) *Who Wants to Be a Millionaire*? Even if your pop culture awareness isn't quiz show material, the title of this chapter alone should have tipped you off that the answer is none other than "d."

The major players involved in *Millionaire* are the American Broadcasting Company, that's ABC in street parlance, Regis Philbin and, of course, people just like you. Deceptively easy, the game grills contestants on their knowledge of everything from cooking and literature to sports and business. To the uninitiated, it seems almost as if fifteen questions are all that separates the contestant from the much-coveted million dollar purse. Of course, when one considers the breadth of topics that those fifteen paltry questions address, that narrow gap begins to look more and more like the Grand Canyon.

No, *Who Wants to Be a Millionaire* is not an easy game. But as freshly minted millionaire John Carpenter recently proved, it is by no means impossible either. The trick lies in learning the rules, figuring out game strategies and expanding your reserve of general knowledge. According to the press release from Michael Davies, the show's executive producer, *Millionaire* is "a general knowledge show in the truest sense. We're not looking for rocket scientists or Ph.D.s. We want real people with a broad range of knowledge and the guts to take risks on what they know and don't know."

Think you got what it takes? Join the club. It's much easier to play from the comfort of your own recliner. Now, if you're really serious about getting inside the winner's circle, take a page from the market researchers and spend a few moments finding out what you're getting yourself into.

IN THE BEGINNING

ABC executives were at their wits' end. Having come in third in the race for ratings yet again, the net had to do something drastic if they wanted to stay in the Big Three along with CBS and NBC. Enter *Who Wants to Be a Millionaire*. Necessity, however, proved less the mother of invention than imitation. *Millionaire* had been making waves in Great Britain for over a year, and was already spreading into countries as far flung as Russia and Australia, when it first aired on ABC on August 16, 1999.

The reasoning went as follows: If the Brits were flocking to the tellie in droves come *Millionaire* night, there was a high probability that Americans would do likewise.

Michael Davies, who now acts as *Millionaire*'s executive producer, has his British roots to thank for the career boost. When the show was first introduced to Britain, Davies was an executive VP at ABC. Fortunately, his many friends and family members in the UK realized the potential of the show and sent him videotaped copies ASAP. No sooner had Davies had a chance to sit through the program, than he was a believer, willing to bet his career on *Millionaire*'s success in the States.

"I watched it and instantly knew four things," he told *Entertainment Weekly*. "This was the best quiz show I had ever seen. The format would work everywhere. I wanted to get it on ABC and get the rights to it . . . And I wanted to quit my job and go produce it."

Davies finally got his wish when he wrested control

of *Millionaire* from the hands of rival bidders. Since the British show was virtually flawless, there was no need to revamp the program for American consumption. The only missing piece to the *Millionaire* puzzle was the host. Current and former talk show hosts such as Phil Donahue, Bob Costas, Regis Philbin and Montel Williams were all under consideration, but no one wanted the gig quite as bad as Regis. "I had to beg, plead, you know, me, the last guy they're thinking about," Regis boasted on *Good Morning America.* "They were still looking for Bill Cullen and somebody else. I had to call out there and beg for the job."

Michael Davies remembers in *Entertainment Weekly* that phone call only too well. "He blew me away with both his passion for the program and his understanding of the format . . . He really wanted it," recalled Davies. "So I thanked him, hung up the phone, and instantly crossed out the other names on the list."

It was that simple. Regis was in and *Millionaire* was officially a part of ABC's lineup. Only August 16, 1999, the date of *Millionaire*'s premiere, would tell whether Michael Davies and ABC executives had been in the right or whether it was the ABC research department's prophecies of doom that had been valid. Since the network had taken England's lead, shuffling around two straight weeks' worth of programming to make room for *Millionaire*, much was riding on the all-important results.

The next day, the through-the-roof ratings were in: 14 million viewers. ABC had a new poster boy in the person of Regis, and the game show biz would never be the same again.

Day after consecutive day, for two weeks running, *Who Wants to Be a Millionaire* trounced the competition. Regis was popping up all over, trumpeting his new slogan "It's hard work saving a network!" And plans to bring the show back come sweeps week were already in the works.

After throttling the rival programs in the sweeps showdown with an estimated viewership of 24 million per night and taking up fourteen spots on the Nielsen's Top Twenty, *Millionaire* was promoted from its position as a seasonal event and installed as a regular, thrice-weekly feature on the ABC lineup.

THE FASTEST FINGER

What is it about *Who Wants to Be a Millionaire* that so captures each nation's imagination? Maybe it's the fact that the rules of the game are so ingeniously simple. Ten contestants are flown into New York City from all over the country to participate in the program's taping. Each takes a seat before their own alphabetized key pad and awaits the Fastest Finger question. After Regis asks the question, options A, B, C, and D appear on the screen and contestants must scurry to put these options in the designated order. The following are two sample Fastest Finger round questions:

1. Put these U.S. state capitals in order from the northernmost to the southernmost.

   A. Springfield
   B. Albany
   C. Baton Rouge
   D. Carson City

2. Put these hit albums in the order they were released, from the most recent to the earliest.

   A. *Rumours*
   B. *Thriller*
   C. *Synchronicity*
   D. *Frampton Comes Alive!*

The contestant who gets the right answer (FYI: that's B, A, D, C for the first one, C, B, A, D for the second one) in the shortest period of time then has the opportunity to play for . . . you guessed it, one million dollars.

As almost anyone, from the producers to the man on the street, will tell you, this is where the real fun begins. The contestant who prevailed in the Fastest Finger round takes his/her place in the hot seat, right across from Regis Philbin. A minute of friendly banter ensues ("What do you do for a living?" "What would you do with a million?"), and then the pressure tactics begin. Each contestant knows that they have to correctly answer all fifteen questions to become a millionaire. Here's the question-by-question monetary breakdown.

Question 1	$100
Question 2	$200
Question 3	$300
Question 4	$500
Question 5	$1,000
Question 6	$2,000
Question 7	$4,000
Question 8	$8,000
Question 9	$16,000
Question 10	$32,000
Question 11	$64,000
Question 12	$125,000
Question 13	$250,000
Question 14	$500,000
Question 15	$1,000,000

THE AMERICAN INQUISITION

Right from the start, a spotlight and ominous music heighten the suspense. Still, the first four ridiculously easy questions (e.g., galoshes are a type of what? A) glove b) boot c) hat d) Polish pancake) rarely pose a problem for most contestants. According to Ann Miller, the show's supervising producer who told *Entertainment Weekly*, "The first four questions are set so the person can relax, catch their breath, and acclimate to the situation."

But as the stakes begin to climb, so apparently does the average contestant's body temperature. The questions start getting harder, the losses more expensive, the lights hotter, and the blasted sound of that ominous music never seems to let up.

After ambling through the $100, $200, $300 and $500 questions, the contestant gets their first taste of the *Millionaire* treatment. Depending on one's areas of expertise, the $1,000 question can be either easy or difficult but, unlike its predecessors, it's not what the village idiot would call common knowledge. Once this question is answered correctly, the contestant is guaranteed at least $1,000 in winnings. Chump change in comparison to the average player's final tally.

At this point, only ten questions separate the contestant from the coveted million. If the contestant answers five more questions correctly (the $2,000, $4,000, $8,000, $16,000, and $32,000), they are guaranteed to walk away with a check for no less than $32,000.

At any time during the game, the contestant can decide that they are satisfied with their total winnings, opt out of answering any more questions and stand down from the hot seat. Why would anyone ever do such a thing, you ask. Well, read on.

In the game of *Millionaire*, $1,000 and $32,000 are the only guarantees. In other words, the only times that a contestant has nothing to lose is when they're faced with the $2,000 and $64,000 questions—if they get these wrong, they don't win the monetary sums, but they get to keep what they've won heretofore. Now, if a contestant answers the $2,000 correctly, but gives the wrong answer to the $4,000 question, they drop all the way back to $1,000 and are sent packing. No big deal? Then just consider this all too probable eventuality, if a contestant answers the $64,000 correctly, but misses on the $125,000, they leave the show with $32,000. The worst case scenario? A contestant who answers the $500,000 question correctly and bites it at the $1 million is out a grand total of $968,000, for they, too, leave with $32,000. So, by answering most of *Millionaire*'s 15 questions, a contestant risks losing thousands, tens of thousands or, yikes, hundreds of thousands of dollars.

Even Regis isn't surprised that so few people actually have the moxie to go for the big win. "You see, if you reach $1,000 . . . you're guaranteed you could leave with that. If you reach $32,000, you're guaranteed to leave with that," he explained on *Good Morning America*. "As you go up to $125,000, and $250,000, you don't want to lose it. And so if you're out of lifelines and you're stuck and you're thinking, 'My gosh, am I going to be reduced to $32,000 or take the $250,000 and leave?' Generally you take the $250,000, unless you've got the courage and the heart of a lion." Well, either that or the bank accounts and stock portfolio of a Forbes.

THROWING LIFELINES

The trauma of the ordeal is lessened only by the existence of the Three Lifelines. Giving hope to all and sundry, these three last resorts are invaluable to every would-be contestant who doesn't know squat about sports or jack about pop culture.

The most popular lifeline, and usually the first to go, is the "Ask the Audience." If stumped or unsure of their answer, every player can ask the 200-strong studio audience for help. Each spectator punches what they believe to be the right answer into their own keyboards and the result of the poll is relayed to the contestant, who has the option to take the audience's word for it, take their winnings and run, or use up yet another lifeline.

The lifeline that comes in second in the popularity

contest is the "Fifty-Fifty," which, aptly enough, leaves the contestant with a fifty percent chance of giving the correct response by eliminating two of the wrong answers.

The third lifeline is called the "Phone a Friend." Every contestant has the opportunity to pick five friends whom they deem knowledgeable enough to save them should push come to shove. When a question pops up, but the right answer remains a blank, contestants have only to tell Regis that they want to call Friend X and the deed is done. The friend then has thirty seconds to listen to the question and give their counsel. Once time is up, they are disconnected and the brunt of the pressure is back on the contestant.

GETTING ON—PART ONE

So far so good, right? Oh, if only it were that easy. Before you can so much as catch a whiff of Regis' suitably expensive eau de cologne, you'll have to suffer through not one, but two rounds of cutthroat competition. These qualifying games are played by phone (in their infinite wisdom, the show's producers have seen fit to waive the phone call's $1.50 price tag), and, in case you're wondering, an element of luck is involved. **However, you can increase your chances of getting on the show if you follow a few basic guidelines**.

1. **Call ahead:** Instead of waiting until the last minute to call, find out the official *Millionaire* number before all the hype begins by logging on to *www.abc.com* and heading over to the *Who Wants to Be a Millionaire* page. Then, don't wait another minute, get on the horn as soon as the phone number is revealed.

2. **Call at odd hours:** The phone lines are open until 3:00 A.M., so the best time to call is late at night, after the rest of the working stiffs have gone to sleep.

3. **Call often:** While *Millionaire* doesn't allow any one person to try for qualification more than once per day, and ensures that you don't go overboard by requesting birth dates and Social Security information, practice can still make perfect. Now that the phone calls are free, some individuals are mastering the technique to their heart's desire by punching in random birth dates and Social Security numbers.

4. **Call prepared:** When you call the *Millionaire* hotline, you will hear Regis's voice and a series of instructions. They will tell you that in order to qualify for the second round, you must answer each of the three questions, posed in order of increasing difficulty, within the ten-second time limit. To accomplish this feat of fast thinking, you will have to take pen and paper in hand and prepare a chart that looks something like this, prior to calling in:

A.	B.	C.
1.	1.	1.
2.	2.	2.
3.	3.	3.
4.	4.	4.

To speed up the answering process, listen to the whole question and all the answers, but write down only the pertinent details.

For instance if the first question you hear is . . .

A. Put the following countries in alphabetical order

1. Argentina
2. Guadamala
3. France
4. Afghanistan

You would write . . .

A. Alphabet

1. Arg
2. Gua
3. Fra
4. Afg

And then quickly punch in 4, 1, 3, 2.

If you enter the correct response in the ten seconds allotted, you will be introduced to the second question.

B. Put the following animated films in the order that they were first released, from the most recent to the earliest.

1. *Lion King*
2. *Beauty and the Beast*
3. *The Little Mermaid*
4. *Tarzan*

The second you hear the question, you would write:

B. recent to early

1. Lion 1993/4
2. B&B 1990/1
3. LitMer 80s
4. Tar 98/99

Then, with the dates at your disposal and the specified order all jotted down, you'd quickly input 4, 1, 2, 3.

Noting the order is of tremendous import, because the tricky quiz masters over at *Millionaire* have a tendency to switch things around a lot. Sometimes they want it chronologically, other times they ask that you work backward. If your answer is correct, you'd get to go on to the third question. Ostensibly the most difficult, this last question isn't always as hard as it's cracked up to be, so don't worry if you get a doozie on the first try, you've still got time and with it more chances to try for a million.

Of course, you might not need more time after all. Provided you get all the answers right, a taped recording of Regis's booming voice will congratulate you on your acumen and you will be asked to input some personal info as well as choose a tape date (a.k.a. the day that you would like to be on the show).

GETTING ON—PART TWO

Here is where the luck factor kicks into high gear. Everyone who made it through the first round on the same day as you will also have to pick a tape date. Your name will then be entered into a drawing with all the other people who answered all their questions correctly *and* picked the same tape date as you. However, and here's the wild card, only a lucky few would-be millionaires will be chosen from the pile of names, contacted the next day and asked to participate in the second qualifying round.

If you survive the drawing, you will receive a phone call from *Millionaire*—stay by the phone, because if you're not in when that phone rings, you're out. A representative (finally, an actual human voice!) will tell you the date and time of the second round, as well as the number to call and your very own pin number.

The second phone call will require that you answer five questions. After this round is over, the pool of possible candidates will be narrowed down to those twelve aspirants (ten contestants and two alternates) who got all the five answers right in the shortest amount of time. The lucky twelve will receive a congratulatory phone call later on that evening, telling them that they and the guest of their choice will be flown to New York for the show's taping. If this should happen to you, be ready to stay for two days, and thank your lucky stars that all accommodations and transportation costs are paid for by *Who Wants to Be a Millionaire*.

Hot Tip: To increase your chances of prevailing in the second round, it's best to call the official *Millionaire* hotline number and name as early a tape date as possible. Because with each passing day, additional people are making it through the first round and getting entered into the competition for your tape date. The less days until your tape date, the less people will have a chance to participate in the combat.

Hot Tip: Just because you made it through round one and survived the drawing doesn't mean that you must stop calling. Why put all your eggs in one basket? Keep calling, and trying for additional chances to win in the final qualifying round.

Hot Tip: By the time the second round is upon you, you should have acquired a facility with working under pressure and punching in the right answers through calling the *Millionaire* hotline repeatedly as described earlier in Step 3 (Call often).

Hot Tip: Two words: speaker phone. Two hands are better than one.

Hottest Tip: Above all, stay calm!!!!!! Answering all the questions correctly should be your top priority. In other words, do not sacrifice the quality of your answers to the speed of response. If we had a quarter for every would-be contestant who knew the right answer but choked under the time pressure and punched in 3, 2, 4, 1 instead of 2, 3, 4, 1, we'd be millionaires ourselves. Don't let this happen to you.

Cheat Sheets: Many of *Millionaire*'s phone-based questions revolve around the holidays and geography. So, if you can find a calendar, a comprehensive list of national holidays and two small, but legible, maps (one of the world, the other of the U.S.), you'll have insured yourself against the horror of drawing a blank at the very last minute.

Totally Unscrupulous Cheater's Tip: Since no one is watching you answer these questions, no one will know if you recruit one or two friends (preferably with interests and hobbies different from your own) to form a *Millionaire* brain trust. Promise to cut your best and brightest pals in on a piece of the action, and ask them to show up at your door come second round phone call time. This ploy will only work if you have more than one phone extension and long telephone cords. Arrange to have both phones next to each for the big call, set your friend up with an answer chart much like your own and let him or her listen in to the recorded questions.

Should you have no idea how to answer a question, look to your brainy friend for support. However, if you're certain that you know what's what, don't waste precious seconds by double-checking your answer.

FASTEST FINGER GAME STRATEGY

Once you're officially on the show, you should remember that *Who Wants to Be a Millionaire*, like any other game, is not without its strategies. To go all the way, or even break $100,000, you've got to know what you're doing. But let's start at the very beginning, with the Fastest Finger competition.

When you're sitting alongside nine other equally revved-up contestants, it's still anybody's game. Of course, there are ways to get a leg up on the competition.

1. **Keep warm:** Reports from the front lines indicate that the *Millionaire* studio is sufficiently frosty to give even the most robust contestant a bad case of temporary rheumatoid arthritis. To keep your joints from getting stiff, wear warm clothes and keep the

blood circulating by flexing your fingers and rubbing your hands together. If you have anything that boasts pockets big enough for your hands and won't embarrass you in front of some 24 million home viewers, you've got a winner.

2. **Know the format:** You'll be sitting in front of a keyboard that looks a lot like this:
A B C D OK

3. **Get it right:** Believe it or not, there are times when only one of the ten contestants gets the right answer. If that person is you, your response time is of no consequence. That hot seat is yours.

4. **The extra step:** Think fast, but most important, don't forget to press "OK." That one extra button has been the death of countless courageous contestants.

5. **Prepare for information overload:** In the qualifying stages, Round One and Round Two, the options are presented one by one over the phone. This makes things considerably easier. But once you get on TV, the plot thickens. All four answers pop up simultaneously. While this may not sound like a big deal of a difference now, just wait until you're on the show. Player beware.

LIFELINES STRATEGY

Knowing how to best implement your lifelines can mean the difference between early retirement and a life on the wrong side of a cubicle. Since you can only use each lifeline once, brushing up on your lifeline pulling skills is a must.

Ask the Audience: According to John Christensen, a contestant who won $16,000 on the show, the audience is "hardly ever wrong on the poll-the-audience lifeline, but the times they have been wrong have all been on higher-level questions. The audience is best polled on matters of pop culture."

Also, if you don't know the answer, keep your thought process private. Take the contestant who had to figure out which toy name means "play well" in Japanese. Faced with options such as yo-yo, Lego, and Atari, this contestant announced that he thought it was either yo-yo or Atari while asking the audience for help all in the same breath. Not wanting to second-guess the man in the hot seat, the audience hardly bothered considering the right answer, Lego.

Fifty-Fifty: Ideally, you would use the Fifty-Fifty at a point when you are debating between two options. In a perfect world, the computer would then rule out one of those two, leaving you confident in the correct answer. While this utopian outcome is the exception rather than the rule, this lifeline has been known to save many contestants from the torments of public humiliation— especially when used on the higher-level questions.

Phone a Friend: Before coming on the show, all finalists and alternates are instructed to submit the phone numbers of five friends/relatives whom they could call upon if they should opt to implement the Phone a Friend lifeline. For optimum effect, these friends should have strengths and interests that are somewhat different from your own. Classify your five friends according to their areas of expertise (i.e., Dad for geography, Mom for history, John for science, etc.), and when a tough question presents itself call the friend whose forte best corresponds to the question category.

Although you can never be sure that your friend will know the answer come crunch time, you can stack the deck in your favor by designating one friend as "the think tank." As supervising producer Ann Miller allowed in *Entertainment Weekly,* "If you have fifteen people in the room and someone shouts out the answer, technically we don't have that as a rule, so that's not cheating."

Tip: If someone is so kind as to help you win a bundle, it's only right that you, in turn, cut them in on a share of the profits (10% should suffice).

GOOD TO KNOW

There's one last thing you should know about *Who Wants to Be a Millionaire*, and that is that you can take forever to answer these questions. You can scratch your head all day if you so choose, and no one can do a damn thing to stop you. "They can take the whole show," Michael Davies affirmed in *Entertainment Weekly*. "We have beautiful editing."

But be warned, if you take too long on any question, you might wind up second-guessing yourself right out of the hot seat. "Take your time," explained Michael Davies. "Read the question. Figure out exactly what we're looking for. Run through the answers very carefully. And go with your original instincts. Often the multiple choice tends to confuse people, when usually they'd instantly know what we're looking for."

Taking a while to answer might come in handy in certain instances. Take, for example, the contestant who decided against answering the $500,000 question that asked how many children were in the *Sound of Music*'s Von Trapp family. Had he only thought back to the song, "Doe, a deer . . . Ray, a drop of golden sun . . ." he might well have remembered that the kids were each given their own note and gone with seven. Then again, he might very well have decided that $250,000 is far too great a sum to risk losing on his limited knowledge of Julie Andrews musicals, and still gone home a rich man.

AND THAT WILL BRING US BACK

So, the big question still remains: what is it about *Millionaire* that made us love it so? Was it just about the money? Or was it about watching regular, everyday people making decisions that could affect the rest of their lives? Staking it all on a hunch, only to cop out when Regis asks, "Is that your final answer?" Agonizing over whether to go with the obvious answer, or whether to trust their gut instinct and go with that little voice in their heads, the little voice that says "Didn't I read something about Santa Fe's altitude being higher than Denver's?"

It's drama, and the only way you can get a taste of it right now is to buy the recently released CD-ROM, log on to *www.abc.com* and work through all the practice games, or call the *Who Wants to Be a Millionaire* hotline and play to win.

CHAPTER TWO

SECRETS OF THE PROS

Imagine getting the opportunity to infiltrate a highly exclusive society, a group that could tell you everything you ever wanted to know about *Who Wants to Be a Millionaire*. Just picture it, you'd not only know your way around the ins and outs, but the odds and ends and all the nooks and crannies that lie in between. In short, you'd have an edge so sharp that it could cut the competition to shreds—even if they are former *Jeopardy* champs who'd won all of Ben Stein's money (not an unusual combination on *Millionaire*).

The fact that *Who Wants to Be a Millionaire* is a totally different show for those who are actively participating than for those who are watching at home shouldn't go without saying, so it won't. Contestants get to see the reality of the show, a side that most viewers could never imagine, much less anticipate. The technical glitches, the waiting periods and the round-the-clock surveillance are just a few of the obstacles with which you'll have to reckon if you are fortunate enough to get on the show.

Those of you who remain confident in your ability to tackle the telephone rounds and make it onto prime time should pay special attention to the experiences of your predecessors. A veritable gold mine of information, former contestants can tell you stories that can make your fortune. Whatever your present level of self-assurance, these are the tales that will ensure that there are no unpleasant surprises come showtime. Believe you us, after you get a call from the show, you'll find that the last thing your nervous system needs is another shock.

WHERE, OH WHERE WILL WE STAY?

Even if you're one of the 9 million who hail from New York City, the home town of *Millionaire*, don't count on spending the night before the show all snug in your own bed. All contestants must fly in the day before the show and stay at a designated hotel. In other words, if your only roomie answers to the name Fluffy and can hear a mailman a mile away, you might want to start looking into some puppy kennels.

But at least you won't have to worry about your own accommodations. *Millionaire*'s producers spare no expense where the talent is concerned. The 1999 contestants stayed in luxury hotels such as the Novotel and the Empire Hotel. "Accommodations were great: the Novotel Hotel, Fifty-second and Broadway, just a few blocks from the studio," former contestant Ken Schwartz told the Game Show Convention Center. "It was a first-class place and certainly nothing I could afford when I visit New York on my own."

NO TIME FOR SIGHTSEEING

Although contestants are warned that they may be required to remain in the city for as long as four days, your stay isn't likely to exceed the one-night minimum unless you make it to the hot seat. The preshow formalities begin the morning after you arrive in New York. All the contestants, alternates, and guests will meet in a hotel room where they'll be briefed on the day's agenda and shuttled en masse to the ABC studios.

"The atmosphere before the show was quite tense," Ken Schwartz revealed. "We arrived at the studio at 12:30 for the 6:30 taping. The entire staff did their best to make people feel relaxed. The green room was filled with food, coffee, snacks, and candy. We were also served a buffet dinner before the show."

While the trip to New York City is billed as *Millionaire*'s major consolation prize, we wouldn't invest in those *Fosse* tickets if we were you. Former contestants maintain that the trip is long on red tape and short on tourist attractions. "We stayed at the Hotel Novotel in Times Square. Pretty decent hotel, great location, but since I didn't have any free time at all, I didn't really get a chance to do anything there," Leszek Pawlowicz lamented.

WHAT'S ALL THIS TALK ABOUT SECURITY?

Thanks to *Millionaire*'s trusty security team, no one is getting their hands on the multimillion-dollar question bank any time soon. Once you get past the studio's titanium gates, you'll be considered a security risk and monitored for the duration of your stay. "You're pretty much told that if someone attempts to talk to you and that person isn't wearing a particular type of badge, you just don't talk to them," $32,000-winner Doug Foster explained to the Game Show Convention Center. "They don't want to run the risk of any security breaches. You have someone with you at all times. Someone eats every meal with you. Someone from the show walks down the hall with you. When you have to go to the bathroom, well, someone from the show follows you to the bathroom. It's about like having the Secret Service with you."

Of course, you might find that being under surveillance isn't without its bright side. According to former players, the production coordinators who are assigned to each contestant are a highly personable lot. "Each contestant is assigned a coordinator who chatted with us at length about our hobbies, embarrassing moments, and what we would do with a million dollars," recalled Ken Schwartz. "This person was also our contact through the day . . . The staff was wonderful. They kept telling us, 'Sure, it's a million dollars but it's only a game show and be proud of getting this far.' They did their job. As dramatic and tense as this game can be, I felt focused and ready to go, not nervous and self-conscious, but still a bit anxious."

PREPARE FOR A WARMUP

Luckily, the six hours that contestants spend in the studio prior to the taping isn't a complete waste of time. Although former contestant Ed Stash has referred to the briefing sessions as "rather standard, the usual legal mumbo-jumbo," there's another, more important aspect to this seemingly interminable waiting period—the practice rounds.

While Ed Stash insists that coming in first in three of the five practice questions "cursed" him for the actual show, there's nothing like a test-run to get the blood circulating. But the Fastest Finger question is only half of the warm-up. Each contestant gets a chance to practice sitting across from Regis and answering the money questions in the hot seat.

IT'S GOOD TO BE REGIS

If there is one thing that all contestants can agree on, it's that Regis Philbin makes for the finest host in all of gameshowland. No steely-eyed plastic man he, Regis positively oozes warmth, vitality and all around bonhomie. In retrospect, hiring the morning talk maestro to helm *Millionaire* was nothing less than a stroke of genius. "I believe Regis genuinely loves this show and lives and dies with the contestants and is one of the keys to its success," said Ken Schwartz. "I don't agree with the criticism about his performance I've heard from some friends and others."

The secret to Regis's appeal is that he constantly goes above and beyond the call of his hosting duties. "Regis, overall, was great," Schwartz enthused. "I've seen several game show tapings in Hollywood where the hosts pay little attention to the contestants during commercials, either wandering off by themselves or remaining behind the podium. Regis, however, chatted with winners during the commercials. His smile seemed to say, 'Don't worry. You're doing great and I wouldn't be surprised if you left here with the whole million.' "

Doug Foster was also won over by Regis's outgoing personality. "Regis was the first host (in my experience) to ever come to the stage for rehearsal with the contestants. He's a real class act. He impressed me as very genuine, supportive, and humorous. I think people realize Regis is truly involved with the contestant in the hot seat. He wants you to do well and look good, because it makes him look good, too."

But there's yet another reason for Regis's universal appeal; unlike the preternaturally gifted Ben Stein and Alex Trebek, Regis is only too fallible. He doesn't have all the answers, and isn't afraid to admit as much. Considering his frequent mispronunciations (all edited out for television, of course), it's fair to say that when Regis innocently asks, "Is that your final answer?" it's not because he's trying to tell you something. "After we finished," recalled $250,000-winner Mark Marcotte, "there were a couple of questions that had to be reshot (my Ooompa-Loompa and Huck Finn questions and John Capolongo's Beatles question) because Regis mispronounced the answers."

In short, whatever critics Regis may have among the viewing public, the contestants who've had a chance to see him live and in color are now fans for life. As Leszek Pawlowicz put it, "Regis was great. Some people have dumped on him, but I think he's a terrific host."

IS THE TAPING ANYTHING LIKE
THE TV SHOW?

From where you're sitting, *Millionaire* probably looks like a pretty action-packed game show. In fact, the televised program is so fast-moving that one hour can seem more like a New York minute. But don't be fooled, this quick pace is more a credit to the editors than to the show or its contestants. The truth is that *Millionaire* takes anywhere from two to four hours to tape. "It's certainly nothing like the show that winds up getting on the air," attested Leszek Pawlowicz. "There's lots of dead spots during the taping (it took a little more than two hours to tape our half-hour episode). They also keep the studio freezing cold."

Ed Stash's taping lasted two hours, but the way he tells it, dead spots had nothing to do with it. "I'd say most of the edits come from narrowing down the time it takes a contestant to answer the questions," he told the Game Show Convention Center. "In our show, though, Doug Van Gundy won the $250K, so there was some setup to get his wife on camera and get some reaction shots. The only real gaffes were Regis having trouble with the pronunciation of some words, like 'Keanu.' Even the audience got into the act to help him out!"

Compounding the waiting periods are the technical realities of *Who Wants to Be a Millionaire*. It was one such factor that managed to unnerve Mark Marcotte. "The true tense moment, though, for me, is what they didn't show you," he told the Game Show Convention Center, "and that's the time when they push out the hot seat. There's some time between when the player shakes hands with Regis and when we actually start playing. The producers talk to you, try to calm you down. That's when it really started to hit me."

Taken as a whole, the lighting, the camera work, the

TelePrompTer, the hot seat, and the host of computer glitches that may or may not beset any given taping, the technical screwups are alone sufficient to extend the proceedings. But figure in the human factor, such as Regis's ongoing battle with pronunciation and the fact that many contestants often take fifteen minutes to answer just one question, and you've got three hours of tape and an editing team that's deserving of an Emmy.

THAT'S ENTERTAINMENT

Much as we like to think of *Millionaire* as a totally fair and impartial quiz show, it's important for future contestants to remember that the show's main priority is not to enrich so much as to entertain. So, sure the show is completely fair, however, impartial it isn't. The producers want to see the most sympathetic characters strike it rich and they can help them do so without so much as bending the rules. Take the story of Doug Foster as an example—if this tale of contestant "tampering" doesn't convince you to hunker down and dig up some interesting factoids for your official contestant bio, nothing will.

"I got on at the very end Saturday night and won $200," Foster recounted. "I went up to the executive producer, Michael Davies, to shake his hand afterward. He told me he could have easily justified ending the show after the previous contestant. They try to put 32 to 35 minutes on tape and edit down to 23. Davies said they had already taped 32 minutes, but after he looked at my bio one more time and one from another contestant, he decided to do one more Fastest Finger round. When I asked him why, he said, 'Because I knew if you or the other guy got on, it would make great television. The story about you and your wife going for the adoption was just too good not to try one more time.'"

Bottom line? *Millionaire* is the ultimate in reality TV. It's about watching a guy who makes $12,500 a year win $250,000. It's about seeing a childless youth minister such as Doug Foster make enough to secure an adoption. It's about you helping yourself by coughing up some drama and getting an extra shot at the hot seat. Any questions?

CHAPTER THREE

THE NEED FOR GREED

If there's one show that can make even *Who Wants to Be a Millionaire* look warm and fuzzy, it would have to be *Greed*. The brainchild of Dick Clark Productions, this show goes straight for the jugular. Just check out the host, Chuck Woolery. Best-known for his long-running stints on *Love Connection* and the *All New Dating Game*, Woolery seems to have finally found an answer to the "for love or money" dilemma in *Greed*. The man is currently on a mission to spread the gospel according to Gordon Gekko through the U.S.

Greed does not mess around. First of all, the ultimate jackpot has been set at a cool $2 million. You won't find any $100, $200, or $300 questions here, the big rewards kick in right away with a $25,000 question. As Chuck Woolery put it, "On *Greed*, we start off with serious money. We're not foolin' around here."

As most people will agree, *Greed* is far too mean to fool around. Why bother building suspense with penny antes and heartbeat music when it's the action itself that's so gosh-darn absorbing. This is the kind of game that starts the process of humiliation off with the first question and goes on to pit the strong against the weak in a fight to the death. Winner take all.

Watching *Greed* gives us all a sense of what it must have felt like to file into the Colosseum, then kick back, relax, and watch some Christians get thrown to the lions back in the heyday of the Roman Empire. For many, that alone is reason enough to tune in.

A KNOCK OFF THE GOLD BLOCK

"A direct ripoff." "A copycat quiz show." "Fox's answer to ABC's megasuccessful *Who Wants to Be a Millionaire.*"

There's no denying the facts, especially when they are this blatant. *Greed* is a ripoff, an obvious attempt to capitalize upon the phenomenal success of *Millionaire*.

That said, who cares?

First of all, *Millionaire* is itself a carbon copy of a preexisting game show. Second, anything that's worth doing is worth doing for twice the money. And last, while some critics may balk at the mercenary nature of this hastily contrived, rush job of a quiz show, *Greed* is anything but a makeshift endeavor.

Now, as to why anyone should give the TV critics so much as a second thought when $2 million are involved, that's anybody's guess.

You gotta give Dick Clark Productions credit. At least they were there, scribbling down the formula and ransacking their right brains, before anyone else could jump on the *Millionaire* bandwagon. Think of *Greed* as the first among equally ratings-hungry knockoffs.

The premier episode took place on November 4, 1999. At this point, mind you, no one knew how *Millionaire* would stack up against the stiff sweeps week competition. Sure, the show had prevailed during the doldrums of summer reruns, but who could have foreseen that it would still be able to carry the day when going head to head with the likes of an all-new *Frasier*? Fox, that's who.

Gambling on *Greed*'s odds of following *Millionaire* all the way to the bank, the Fox execs cleared their prime-time schedule of a spate of underperformers to make way for the show that differed from *Millionaire* only in that it used teams instead of single contestants, gave away $2 million instead of one and was helmed by slick game show titan Chuck Woolery instead of everybody's friend and affable next-door-neighbor Regis Philbin. And what do you know, but it worked. *Millionaire* had whetted America's long-dormant appetite for quiz shows, but it was *Greed* that really satisfied.

Fox garnered the kind of ratings they hadn't seen since *Ally McBeal*, and additional installments of the show were immediately ushered into production. The hunt for contestants was on, and there was no end to the willing men and women lining up for a piece of the American Dream.

To date, no one has won the $2 million grand prize. Not surprisingly, most people are neither brave nor foolish enough to stake a hundred thousand dollars on their knowledge of trivia. The good news is that on November 18, 1999, three contestants did have the opportunity to split one million three ways. The bad news is that one of the said three pulled a double or nothing, and nearly passed out on stage upon learning that he'd be going home with the latter.

GREED IS GOOD?

Any show that starts off by arbitrarily eliminating one of six contestants has got to be the product of a diabolical mind. Imagine the effects that such a crushing blow might have upon the spirits of the solitary loser. Since each of the six contestants has an 83% chance of competing for the prize money, the totally unexpected defeat could very well convince the odd-man-out that they are, at the very least, cursed for life. Worse yet, imagine the pain of coming home and facing your friends and family after just such a debacle. Suddenly, you're the kid who eats paste and no one wants to sit next to you on the school bus. Soul-crushing.

The only consolation to *Greed*'s unfortunate castaways is that the qualifying question is invariably something trivial, and not knowing the answer is by no means an indictment of one's overall intelligence. For instance, how many average-sized licks does it take to get to the bottom of a Tootsie Pop? Let's pretend the correct answer was 147. The person who came closest to this number would get to be the team captain. The four runners-up would get to be contestants/teammates. The person who was furthest away from the magic number wouldn't get so much as a pat on the back.

After spending the commercial break in lamenting the sorry lot of *Greed*'s first unwitting victim (or, as the case may be, triumphing over the comeuppance handed over to that smug law school grad), you are introduced to the remaining contestants. Here is your chance to find out what they'd do with $2 million. Exciting, no?

Well, maybe not yet. The real thrills lie in watching the contestants make their way up the money tree, or as its officially called, drumroll please . . .

THE TOWER OF GREED

Off to the side of Chuck Woolery sits a grand display of wealth, wealth that can be yours for the spending provided you have the right answers. The gradations are as follows:

1. $25,000
2. $50,000
3. $75,000
4. $100,000
5. $200,000
6. $500,000
7. $1,000,000
8. $2,000,000

For some time the jackpot was set to grow by a whopping $50,000 each day that the top prize remained unclaimed, and it was not at all unusual for the uppermost rung to actually exceed the $2 million mark. The producers have since reconsidered their generosity, and fixed the jackpot at $2 million.

The Tower of Greed is the focal point of this quiz show. Every right answer brings the contestants one notch closer to the big payoff. The first round of questions are straightforward multiple choice. But unlike on *Millionaire, Greed*'s questions are more pop culture than erudition. "What is the most common reason that people give for logging on to the Internet?" (Hint: it's neither for the stock quotes nor for the chat rooms. If you're thinking e-mail, you're right.) "Which of the following personalities is a rapper?"(Dr. Drew? Don't think so. Dr. Doctor? Yeah, right. The obvious answer is Dr. Dre.) "What city is headquarters for both CNN and Coca-Cola?" (New York isn't even an option. Atlanta is the answer.)

Contestants take turns answering questions. The first one goes to contestant number four, the next one goes to number three, and so on until all four of the initial questions have been answered or a wrong response is given. Of the first round of questions, the first two come with four answers (e.g., What is the main color on a box of Crayola crayons? a) black b) red c) yellow d) orange), while the second two attempt to confound the contestants with five options (What is the second most popular holiday for gift-giving? a) Easter b) Valentine's Day c) Sweetest Day d) Mother's Day e) Father's Day).

While the captain is relieved of the responsibility of answering these particular brain teasers, s/he has ultimate veto power. Whenever s/he so desires, the captain can disagree with and alter any answer given by a mere team member. The captain is also entrusted with the grave responsibility of deciding for the whole team whether to take the winnings and run or to follow the need for greed further up the tower.

No doubt *Millionaire* is the kinder, gentler quiz show. One viewing of *Greed* and you'll see that despite its rather obtuse line of questioning, this show makes winning a great deal more challenging. First of all, there are no lifelines. As for guarantee points, forget about it. If your team wins $200,000 and then misses on the $500,000 question, everyone goes home empty-handed. Neither do the folks at *Greed* see any reason to show the team captain the question prior to letting him/her decide whether or not to proceed. It's a dog-eat-dog world, and *Greed* isn't about to throw anyone a bone.

The immensity of the pressure that's exerted upon the captain is outweighed only by the aggravation of the team members who want to stop when the captain says go, or vice versa. Leave it to *Greed* to somehow work a hierarchy into game shows.

And let's not even get started on what happens when a captain overrides a correct answer. We're just guessing here, but something tells us that there is nothing so brutal as the fury of *Greed* contestants scorned.

THE TERMINATOR

If you have yet to make the *Greed*-Pure Evil connection, this next point may fill in the blanks. After the first round of questions has been answered, a thunderous sound of impending doom fills the contestants with dread as the arrival of "The Terminator" is announced. Flashing lights then begin to light up the contestants' podiums. Like a ball on a roulette wheel, the lights travel from one contestant to the next, and where they'll stop nobody knows.

The chosen team member, a.k.a. The Terminator, now has the opportunity to either forget the whole thing or to challenge a fellow teammate to a duel to the death, a one-question standdown that will ensure the elimination of either The Terminator or the opponent. Even the most altruistic contestants, the sort of bleeding hearts that might have planned to allocate every last dime of their winnings to ending world hunger and effecting world peace, cannot resist the temptation to go for a showdown.

First and foremost is the cash money incentive. As every contestant well knows, the fewer team members, the "more for me!" *Greed* further encourages this way of thinking by giving the victor of The Terminator challenge what would have been the loser's piece of the pie (translation: each of the original five contestants is due to get 20% of the pot, if one contestant terminates another, that contestant stands to net 40%). Now, if that isn't provocation enough, Chuck Woolery immediately offers the would-be Terminator a $10,000 wad of cash (more if the team has already won a lot of money) in exchange for agreeing to face off with a fellow teammate. So simply by calling out another contestant, The Terminator is guaranteed to go home at least $10,000 richer, win or lose.

Then there's the studio audience. Playing the part of the little devil on the left shoulder to perfection, members of the audience are vociferous in urging The Terminator to "do it."

But wait, there's yet another upshot to turning on your fellow man. The Terminator gets to pick his opponent. Here's where the gloves come off and there isn't a Mr. Nice Guy to be found for miles around. In the history of *Greed*, no Terminator has ever picked on somebody they honestly believed to be as smart or smarter than themselves. Dippy-looking contestants with low-prestige jobs are The Terminators' first victims. Chuck Woolery might as well ask The Terminator to stand up and announce who they believe to be the most dim-witted contestant on the panel.

All told, it's an ugly business. Which isn't to say that it's not great TV. Who doesn't like to see a struggle of David and Goliath proportions? Better yet, who out there isn't rooting for the underdog to win?

Most of *Greed*'s die-hard adherents will agree that

The Terminator is the show's *pièce de résistance*. Appearing as many as four times during a single game, it is this feature that makes the existence of a single $2 million winner a distinct, albeit unlikely, possibility.

Take Heed: If the frequency with which challengers fall prey to their opponents teaches us anything, it's to never underestimate the little guy—and to think twice before taking Chuck Woolery up on his $10,000 offer.

SECOND-DEGREE BURN

The first round of questioning implies the existence of a second round. To keep things interesting, the creators of *Greed* have seen fit to change the format of the higher grossing questions. Instead of the standard multiple-choice format, the $200,000 question gives contestants a question that has six possible answers, four of which are correct.

Example: Which are the four highest grossing movies in the history of cinema?

1. *ET: The Extra-Terrestrial*
2. *Star Wars: The Phantom Menace*
3. *Star Wars*
4. *Jurassic Park*
5. *Titanic*
6. *Independence Day*

Every team member has a chance to weigh in with their verdict. Unless they'd spent the last four years exploring the Australian Outback, the first contestant would automatically go for the obvious right answer, in this case *Titanic*. Then the controls would be handed over to the next team member, and so on until all four answers had been given and either approved or substituted by the team captain.

If the contestants give the correct responses (in this particular case they'd be ruling out *ET* and *Star Wars*), then the game continues with Chuck Woolery turning to the team captain and asking, "Do you want to keep the cash, or do you feel the need for greed?" If, however, so much as one choice has been off the mark, all participating parties leave with nothing except the shirts on their backs.

Of course, even *Greed* isn't all bad. At the $200,000 level and above, the show offers each team one Freebie—in layman's terms, an opportunity to automatically eliminate one wrong answer. But one Freebie is all they get, use it once and it's gone for good.

The urge to retrieve the lost Freebie often hits contestants right around the time they hear the $500,000 question, which also requests four correct answers, but gives a possible seven options instead of the six that accompanied the foregoing question. The $1 million question again asks for the four right responses, while overwhelming the contestants with eight choices.

ON THE OUTS

Considering the difficulty rating of the upper-echelon questions, it is only fair of the producers to give the team members a helping hand. While they don't go so far as to reveal the question prior to letting the captains decide whether to further scale the Tower of Greed or to go home with their winnings, they do let the team in on the question category. These categories run the gamut from movies to computers to popular food. To be perfectly honest, however, such broad headings are rarely of any assistance.

Since the categories aren't of much use, *Greed* does something else to prove that it is not, in fact, the black sheep of game shows. After the team members lock in their choices, Chuck Woolery checks each answer one by one. After three of the four choices have been deemed correct, Woolery gives the captain an out. At the $200,000 level, the out is worth $20,000, to be divvied up among the teammates. At the $500,000 level, the out is $50,000. It is at the rare and elusive $1 million level, however, that *Greed* starts to get creative. The last time this level was attained, Woolery offered each contestant a 2000 Jaguar XK-8 and $25,000 before letting them see whether their fourth answer was correct. At this lofty plateau, contestants are allowed to decide individually whether they want to take the out and renounce their share of the winnings or risk it all for a chance at the hundreds of thousands.

Oddly enough, it almost seems as if this show doesn't want you to win. Fortunately, all of the foregoing contestants were gunning for the big bucks and chose to shrug off the cash and cars. The reward for their valor was $1 million. The ratings that night were some of the highest in *Greed*'s brief history.

THE $2 MILLION KAMIKAZE

No guts, no glory? The cautious majority of *Greed* contestants would beg to differ. Risking 80, 60, 40, or even 20 percent of $1 million to go for $2 million is simply too rich for most people's blood. As of this writing, only one man has lived to tell the tale of his losing battle with *Greed*'s most feared and revered question.

At this stage of the game, the captain usually loses his leadership stripes as contestants are finally allowed to make up their own minds. As if to corroborate the hypothesis that the producers of *Greed* do not want anyone laying their grubby paws on the two mill, the final question does not allow for an out. Once a contestant decides to go for the double platinum, they are locked in. They have to answer and cannot back out for a consolation prize at any point whatsoever. So, as you can well see, it's not for nothing that Chuck Woolery proudly calls *Greed* "the most dangerous game in America."

Only Daniel Avila, the man who scaled the Tower of

Greed all the way to its perilous peak, knows what it is to stare such danger in the eye. After taking his team to the previously unsurpassed $1 million mark, Avila was left holding 20% of the pot, $200,000, while his two remaining teammates, Curtis and Melissa, had terminated their way into the 40% bracket and were sitting mighty pretty on $400,000 a piece. All had the opportunity to play on. The category was "Odors," the payoff was $2.2 million, the risk for Curtis and Melissa was $400,000. They wisely declined the offer.

Avila, however, had a better idea. Sensing that his better-off teammates would balk at the prospect of going on, he knew that if he were to stake his $200,000, the $2.2 million at the end of the rainbow would be his, all his. Having shown himself to be a risk taker throughout the program—forcing his teammates to carry on to $500,000 and then $1 million when he knew full well that they felt more than well compensated at the $500,000 level—Avila was not about to back down from the formidable challenge.

"I wanted to go for the jackpot," he explained to the Game Show Convention Center. "My main concern was what Melissa or Curtis would do. If one or both stayed, then we would share the jackpot but there would also be another Terminator! However, we would be collaborating on the final answer. But I was certain the two of them would take the $400K and leave. In fact if I had had $400K I probably would have left, too. But everything was set up for me to try for the jackpot.

"Yes, $200K (before taxes) is a lot of money," he continued. "I do not have $200K or even $100K. But a $2.2 million jackpot can be life-changing. I would always wonder for the rest of my life whether I could have answered that question. I didn't want to wonder 'what if?' I wasn't thrilled with the category, but I knew it would be four out of nine. I figured a couple of the answers could be discarded and I would then have a smaller group from which to pick my four answers. I knew there would be only thirty seconds. I knew I could not change my answers. I knew there would be no buy-out if I answered three correctly."

Given all these deterrents, Avila held fast to his dream. As his erstwhile team members looked on from the wings, he stood alone before the merciless Tower of Greed, the very image of man confronted with the sublime, and goaded the powers that be to bring it on. What followed is forever ingrained in the hearts and minds of avid *Greed*-viewers everywhere.

"According to Yale University, which four of these smells are the most recognizable?"

1. Baby powder
2. Peanut butter
3. Mothballs
4. Tuna
5. Coffee
6. Dry cat food
7. Chocolate
8. Cinnamon
9. Vicks VapoRub

Choosing tuna, peanut butter, coffee and Vicks VapoRub, Avila knew that the matter was now in the hands of fate. Peanut butter . . . correct! Coffee . . . correct! Vicks VapoRub . . . correct! With no way to back out and his entire future hinging on the unmistakable musk de tuna, the final verdict came back as . . . incorrect. As anyone from Hershey, Pennsylvania probably knows, the last of the big four was chocolate.

Final score: *Greed*—$2.2 million, Avila—$0

"What can I say? I came close," shrugged Avila. "I have the fame but no fortune. But I tell people no one is ever going to offer me that kind of money to answer *one* question. As Curtis said, 'It's a no brainer.' "

QUALIFYING QUESTION STRATEGIES

While *Greed* might have got the better of Daniel Avila, learning from his mistakes and those of countless other contestants can help you avoid falling into the same snares. Since your first opportunity to slip up comes during the qualifying question round, lets assess this answering strategy first.

Of the twenty qualifying questions that have been handed down in 1999, only three have dealt with percentages. Since the answer to these is always between one and one hundred, common sense must be your guide. Pay close attention to the wording of the question, look for clues about the answer, and respond accordingly.

Hot Tip: Your best bet on the percentage questions is to avoid the extremes. Even if you think the number is very high or very low, it is unwise to enter a guess that is either above 65% or below 25%—unless of course the question is "What percentage of American adults believe in Santa Claus?"

But percentage-based questions make up only a small portion of the qualifying questions pool. Most likely, you'll be asked a question with a response that ranges anywhere from one to 1,000 (How many rooms in the White House? How many spaces on a Scrabble board? How many dreams does the average person remember in a year?). In such cases, you'll have to defer to your logical reasoning skills yet again.

Hot Tip: If, however, you are presented with a question that leaves you with absolutely no idea (How many hours does the average woman cry in a lifetime? How many crayons has the average North American child used by age 10?) our suggestion is that you go with 200. While this may sound a little bit arbitrary, like the people who insist you to pick C when in doubt on a multiple choice quiz, the history of *Greed* shows that 200 is indeed the number most likely to get you on the team. In fact, according to our calculations, answering 200 to all of the non-percentage oriented questions would have worked fifteen out of seventeen times. While these are not bad odds, this tip is still only to be used in case of emergency.

TERMINATOR STRATEGIES

As mentioned earlier, unless you've decided that $10,000 is a sufficiently large prize, entering into The Terminator challenge lightly is ill advised. The truth is that most contestants do not attempt a termination unless they are looking to increase their share of the loot. Also, keep in mind that there is far more shame in agreeing to play The Terminator than in declining.

Now, if you're absolutely intent to jump on any and all Terminator opportunities that come your way, the strategy is threefold. First and foremost, think of the cash. If you've been chosen as The Terminator, and someone has already terminated their way into owning more than one-fifth of the pie, your mark is set. After all, why risk it all for a mere two-fifths when you can walk away with three-fifths?

Next, think of the team and the implications that your actions can have on overall winnings down the line. If you terminate a key player, your team's chances of winning big have just grown that much smaller. This is certainly why the weakest links are usually the first to go. Now, if you look around and decide that keeping the team in tact would considerably increase your chances of making it to the big leagues, maybe this isn't the best time to abuse your Terminator's privileges.

Finally, when you've picked your opponent, put your hand to your buzzer, and prime your ears for the question, it's to your advantage to buzz in first. But please, don't forget to listen to the whole question. "Remember to listen to the entire question, unlike what James did in the first Terminator," Daniel Avila advised would-be contestants on Game Show Guide. "James was a Website designer. Melissa challenged him and even though he buzzed in first he forgot what the question was about. All he heard was Pentium and computer. He blurted out Compaq. The question was basically who made the chip. Intel, of course!"

GENERAL STRATEGIES

The truth is that you can't cram your way into the $2 million jackpot. Preparation for *Greed* takes a lifetime of learning and an aptitude for taking tests. "As with most game shows, there's no way to really prepare," Daniel Avila told the Game Show Convention Center. "I have a broad educational background in the humanities. I also have the knack of recalling trivia. I also read a lot. I know a little bit about a lot of things. I did check my almanac after I was called to be on the show . . . But there is almost no way to try to outguess the writers on this show."

Of course, you can try to figure out where the writers are going with the question. Oftentimes, the clues are encrypted into the questions themselves. Take for instance the $100,000 question that asked, "According to an AOL poll, what do 80% of Americans believe is the most important invention of the twentieth century?" The possible answers were television, air conditioner, computer, jet airplane, and microwave oven. All important developments, but the team chose television. Had the question been asked by CNN, that response might very well have been correct. Unfortunately, AOL had come up with another answer. Can you guess which it was?

To further increase your chances of winning at *Greed*, you'll have to have an instinct for eliminating the obviously wrong answers. Even if you aren't sure of the correct response, you can usually narrow your options down to two possible answers. This technique should alleviate a great deal of confusion, allow you to focus on the most important aspects of the question and more than double your chances of giving the right response.

In the end, however, there's really only one way to ready yourself for *Greed*, and that's to hope for the best and prepare for the worst. "I would familiarize myself with the rules of the game. And one has to be prepared to accept the risks as well as the rewards," explained Avila. "You could end up not qualifying for the five-person team. You could get a captain who either won't change a wrong answer or changes a correct one. You could also have a captain quit after four questions. Or you could end up with a gung-ho captain who seems determined to either win big or lose it all. And you must also be prepared to accept the fact there is the chance you will be terminated."

Keeping all this in mind, there are yet a few more things you'll need to know if you still want to be on *Greed*.

GETTING ON

If you think that scaling the Tower of Greed is this show's greatest challenge, you obviously haven't tried your hand at becoming a contestant. Talk about your Herculean feats, getting on the show is well-nigh impossible. In fact, nearly all of the 1999 contestants had been hand-picked by *Greed*'s producers from a pool of former game show contestants. That's right, most of the people whom you watched in the show's first season were old pros who'd already played and won on such erudite quiz shows as *Win Ben Stein's Money* and *Jeopardy*.

But who can blame the producers? They were, after all, in a race to beat the clock. *Greed* had to go on in November, and after working out all the rules, hiring the host, and trying to forestall any technical difficulties, who had time for something as trivial as widespread contestant searches?

Most of the contestants were called directly by the show, and had only to pass a test to qualify. "The test was just like the show in terms of multiple choice answers," Avila revealed on Game Show Guide. "The window of testing was very small. I took the test the Saturday before the first taping day, which was the following Tuesday."

These questionable practices were soon to come to an end. After Fox picked up *Greed* as a regularly scheduled program, the nationwide search for contestants was on. While the show still reserved the right to pilfer its contestants from past game shows, all legal residents of the U.S. who were 18 or older were invited to either call or mail in their entries by December 9, 1999. While people were limited to two $1.99 calls per day, there was no ceiling for mail-in entries.

Unlike on *Millionaire*, however, the winners of this initial round were not chosen for their merit so much as their sheer luck. A random drawing was held, and 250 names were chosen from the total mailed-in and phoned-in entries. Those fortunate enough to land on the list got a phone call from the show. Those who weren't at home were immediately dropped from the competition. The rest were dubbed qualifying entrants and given the opportunity to talk to a *Greed* representative and answer a series of knowledge-based, multiple-choice questions, all while having their personality judged on the basis of "charm, communication skills, and sense of humor."

The twenty-five qualifying entrants who passed the test and were deemed most all-around charming were flown to Los Angeles (sans companion) and thrown into a contestant pool. And still, no promises were made. The winners of the contest search were duly informed that there was still a chance that they would not be chosen to play on *Greed*, and that even if they were chosen to play, their segment might not be taped. Furthermore, even if their show was taped, there was still a very real likelihood of their segment winding up on the cutting room floor.

If you're still stuck on the notion of competing for $2 million, the contestant hotline is 1-800-498-2077. You can also check out the *Greed* Websites at *www.fox.com* and *www.greedtv.com*. Good luck.

THE UGLIEST AND MOST PAINFUL MOMENTS IN THE HISTORY OF *GREED*

"Why?!" If a comedy of bad manners is what you're after, forget what you've heard about *Cops* and don't even think of turning to the guests on *Jerry Springer*. Pound for pound, no show can so much as approximate the blunders and cold-blooded backbiting that are the trademark of *Greed*. For the ultimate in savagery, look no further than the show's single biggest winner to date, Curtis Warren.

Warren is proof positive that you don't get to the top without stepping on a few poor, trusting souls. After working his way all the way up to the $1 million mark, Warren had the opportunity to terminate one of his teammates and pocket their hard-won $200,000 share of the winnings. He didn't think twice before picking and terminating Jackie, whose stunned and plaintive "Why?!" pretty much said it all.

Some Captain! In every game show, there's bound to be that moment when a contestant confidently goes where no sensible life-form would ever follow. Sadly, this is one show where a contestant can easily drag their whole team down with them. The one that stands out as the very worst of these case scenarios occurred at the $200,000 level. The question read: "Which of these products are found in the most U.S. households? 1. television 2. radio 3. VCR 4. personal computer 5. home CD player 6. answering machine.

The answers given by the contestants were television, radio, VCR, and, of course, the answering machine. It could have been so beautiful. Each of the contestants could have walked away with at least $40,000. But the captain had to pull rank. Invoking his veto privilege, he made short work out of changing answering machine (average price: $15) to personal computer (average price: $1,000), and, in so doing, lost the game while his helpless team looked on in absolute horror.

WHAT YOU WANT TO KNOW

1. *How much behind-the-scenes communication is there between contestants?*
   Interaction between contestants who are destined for the same team is discouraged. Producers do not want loyalty, camaraderie, or the spirit of good sportsmanship fouling up the perfect blend of treachery and betrayal that is *Greed.*

2. *What is Chuck Woolery really like?*
   "I liked Chuck Woolery," Dan Avila told the Game Show Convention Center. "He was friendly on the set. I'm the only contestant he could interact with. He seemed to have a soothing effect on me. And I think he wanted us to get the answers correct and to win. I've always thought he is a good host."

3. *Who is* Greed's *single-biggest winner?*
   Actually, the Champion of Greed title is presently being shared by two contestants, Curtis Warren and Melissa Shirvo. After eliminating a contestant a-piece, each won $410,000 on the November 11, 1999, show. Melissa Shirvo is an actress in New York City, while Curtis Warren is an air traffic controller from Cathedral City, California.

4. *Where can I find transcripts of past shows?*
   Surf to *http://jelliott.homepage.com/games/about-greed.html*

You can search the official *Greed* Websites all you want, but if attention to detail and copious notes are what you're after, this page has it all, stats, transcripts, contestant information, and much more.

5. *Are the cash prizes awarded in lump sums?*
   Leave the $1 million paychecks to *Who Wants to Be a Millionaire*. Contestants who win $200,000 or more on *Greed* are paid in annuities of $100,000 per year.

6. *How much money has* Greed *awarded so far?*
   As of this writing, *Greed* has aired eight times and awarded a total of $3,630,000.

NEW ARRIVALS

The game show pond has suddenly grown a lot more crowded. And, wouldn't you know it, but the new crop of televised quizzes all have one thing in common—the promise of a six-figure giveaway. Although it's still too early to say whether these shows will have what it takes to stay the course set by *Who Wants to Be a Millionaire*, they are bound to produce several big winners before the cancellation curtain falls. So if you don't want to put all your eggs in Regis's basket, consider the following sampling of the shows that would be *Millionaire*.

1. *Twenty-One* (NBC)—Two contestants, two soundproof isolation booths, one host in the person of daytime talk show host Maury Povich, and a storied, if checkered, past that is bound to draw viewers by the millions.

   Twenty-One gained tremendous popularity in the 1950's, when it was *the* show to beat. Back then, the questions were impossible and the viewers naive. The show's winning streak began in September, 1956, and ended amid the scandal of a congressional probe in October, 1958, when it was revealed that the hermetically sealed envelopes containing the all-important questions were a fraud. Robert Redford's 1994 film *Quiz Show* is based upon how the ratings-hungry producers manipulated the show by leaking questions to contestants.

What with the new policy of fair play, not to mention the much-touted "dumbing down" of America, the new *Twenty-One* boasts multiple-choice questions that should enable a good quarter of the population to play along at home. There is also a lightning round that consists of true/false questions and an intriguing Internet component. The object of the game, as ever, is to be the first contestant to get to twenty-one points, or $210,000. Each point is worth $10,000 and contestants can choose questions that are worth anywhere from one to ten points apiece (of course, the eleven-pointer is likely to be a stumper). Final per-game earnings are the winner's cash total minus their opponent's cash total. Triumphant contestants get to come back after each win, so the jackpot can very well extend into the millions.

Getting on the show is as simple as calling the periodically announced contestant hotline (go to *www.nbc.com* for more info), and answering 15 questions. The second qualifying round requires an in-person 30-question audition.

2. *Winning Lines* (CBS)—This show also comes to us courtesy of the U.K. The host is the eternally youthful Dick Clark and the players are the Forty-niners. That's right, there are 49 contestants in the first round of competition. Questions with numerical responses are fired off ("How many black dots are there on a pair of dice?" "If you wanted to give each member of the Backstreet Boys a regular

pack of Wrigley's gum, how many individual pieces of gum would you be giving them?") and contestants have fifteen seconds to figure out whether the answer corresponds to their number. If they buzz in incorrectly, they are out. If they don't buzz in at all, they are out. Only if they buzz in correctly do they get to remain for round two.

The second round features six surviving players and changes the rules to speed things up. Although the questions are still numerical in nature, everyone gets a shot at answering. If one contestant correctly answers a question that corresponds to another contestant's number, the latter contestant is out. This continues until just one contestant remains. The final one-person round seems more like a punishment than a prize. To walk away the better for the experience, the so-called winner must answer as many questions as possible within the space of three minutes. While the U.S. prizes have yet to be announced, the Queen's version offers a top prize of a three-week around-the-world vacation (or holiday, as the Brits call it).

If you're still interested, call 1-800-264-7979 to qualify.

3. *Survivor!* (CBS)—Also known as "People Would Do Anything to Be on TV." Originating in Sweden, this hard-knocks show deposits sixteen contestants in the wilderness of a remote, uninhabited island in the South China Sea. The contest continues for six weeks as cameras follow the contestants from one wilderness survival challenge to the next. Trials include such traditional Swiss Family Robinson rituals as foraging for food, warding off poisonous snakes and wild boars, building shelters, and trying desperately to remain sane.

Every three days, the contestants hold a popularity contest to eliminate one drain on their collective resources. Finally, when only two survivors remain on the island, the exiled contestants vote for their favorite to stay. The loser of this poll leaves the isle, while the winner remains to collect $1 million.

All told, *Survivor!* might be a fun show to watch, but we wouldn't want to visit. If you do, be prepared to sign away your legal rights to the producers and to endure a battery of intensive psychological and physical tests. This show is dangerous, and it's not taking any chances—that's your job.

PART II

TEST YOUR TRIVIA KNOWLEDGE

Are You Ready to Win Some Big Money? Let's Find Out!

CHAPTER FOUR

ENTERTAINMENT

1. In what year were the Beatles formed?

    A. 1965
    B. 1961
    C. 1959
    D. 1957

2. What instrument does Woody Allen play in the film *Wild Man Blues*?

    A. Clarinet
    B. Bassoon
    C. Trumpet
    D. Harmonica

3. What is the longest-running series in television history?

    A. *M*A*S*H*
    B. *Seinfeld*
    C. *Little House on the Prairie*
    D. *Gunsmoke*

4. What movie star is the focus of the most biographies?

    A. Marilyn Monroe
    B. Natalie Wood
    C. Charlie Chaplin
    D. Greta Garbo

5. What is the highest grossing film in history?

   A. *ET*
   B. *Titanic*
   C. *Star Wars*
   D. *Jurassic Park*

6. What famous daughter did Michael Jackson wed in 1994?

   A. Nancy Sinatra
   B. Lisa Marie Presley
   C. Carrie Fisher
   D. Jane Fonda

7. On what TV show did Jackie Gleason appear in before finding a permanent home on the *Honeymooners*?

   A. *The Ed Sullivan Show*
   B. *I Love Lucy*
   C. *Cavalcade of Stars*
   D. *Leave It to Beaver*

8. Which of the following is *not* a Woody Allen film?

   A. *Bullets over Broadway*
   B. *Radio Days*
   C. *Metropolitan*
   D. *Manhattan*

9. What actress was quoted as saying, "You never really know a man until you have divorced him"?

   A. Elizabeth Taylor
   B. Katherine Hepburn
   C. Marilyn Monroe
   D. Zsa Zsa Gabor

10. Which television family did not launch a recording career?

   A. The Bradys
   B. The Partridge family
   C. The Osmonds
   D. The Cleavers

11. What game is a required part of a course on financial accounting at Indiana University?

   A. Othello
   B. Monopoly
   ·C. Life
   D. Uno

12. Which relationship advice book advises couples to "Give four hugs a day."

   A. *Light His Fire*
   B. *Men Are from Mars, Women Are from Venus*
   C. *Love or Perish*
   D. *Dating for Dummies*

13. Who wrote the best-selling book that served as the basis for the twelve-hour drama *Roots*?

   A. Sidney Sheldon
   B. Stephen King
   C. Alex Haley
   D. Toni Morrison

14. What actor portrayed Lieutenant Colonel Henry Blake on the TV-series *M*A*S*H*?

   A. Harry Morgan
   B. McLean Stevenson
   C. Alan Alda
   D. Bill Christopher

15. Who is the first character to speak in *Star Wars*?

   A. C3PO
   B. Luke Skywalker
   C. Princess Leia
   D. Obi-Wan Kenobi

16. What substance was used for blood in the famous shower scene in Alfred Hitchcock's movie *Psycho*?

   A. Ketchup
   B. Kool-Aid
   C. Chocolate syrup
   D. Maple syrup

17. What model introduced the waif look in 1966?

   A. Twiggy
   B. Cheryl Tiegs
   C. Patty Hanson
   D. Kate Moss

18. What movie saw the first teaming of Walter Matthau and Jack Lemmon?

   A. *The Odd Couple*
   B. *Grumpy Old Men*
   C. *The Fortune Cookie*
   D. *Out to Sea*

19. What book was the film *Apocalypse Now* based on?

   A. *Lord Jim*
   B. *Heart of Darkness*
   C. *Lord of the Flies*
   D. *A Separate Peace*

20. Which of the following is *not* a John Lennon album?

   A. *Imagine*
   B. *Mind Games*
   C. *Double Fantasy*
   D. *Mirage*

21. What American director is buried in an olive orchard on a ranch owned by his friend, matador Antonio Ordonez in Sevilla, Spain?

   A. Orson Welles
   B. Alfred Hitchcock
   C. Cecil B. Demille
   D. Charlie Chaplin

22. What cartoon featured characters named after Renaissance painters?

   A. Power Rangers
   B. Teenage Mutant Ninja Turtles
   C. Teletubbies
   D. Pokémon

23. What supermodel was quoted as saying, "I don't get out of bed for less than $10,000"?

   A. Kate Moss
   B. Cindy Crawford
   C. Christie Brinkley
   D. Linda Evangelista

24. What TV news-magazine earned 63 Emmys since it first aired in 1968?

   A. *Dateline*
   B. *60 Minutes*
   C. *48 Hours*
   D. *20/20*

25. Where did the Ricardos and the Mertzes relocate to in the sixth season of *I Love Lucy*?

    A. California
    B. Florida
    C. New York
    D. Connecticut

26. *The Colbys* was a short-lived spinoff of what night-time soap?

    A. *Dynasty*
    B. *Dallas*
    C. *Knots Landing*
    D. *Soap*

27. How much did Columbia pictures pay for the rights to the Broadway musical *Annie*?

    A. $500,000
    B. $1 million
    C. $5 million
    D. $9 million

28. How many writers worked on the screenplay for the 1994 film *The Flintstones*?

    A. 2
    B. 8
    C. 12
    D. 32

29. First founded in 1889 in Japan, what did the Nintendo company originally manufacture?

    A. Playing cards
    B. Board games
    C. Pool tables
    D. Darts

30. What television show didn't feature a single girl living on her own in a big city?

    A. *Suddenly Susan*
    B. *Time of Your Life*
    C. *Growing Pains*
    D. *Felicity*

31. What is the only PG-rated animated Disney film?

    A. *Sleeping Beauty*
    B. *The Black Cauldron*
    C. *The Lion King*
    D. *Cinderella*

32. Which *Friends* star was originally hired to portray Roz on *Frasier*?

    A. Courtney Cox
    B. Lisa Kudrow
    C. Jennifer Aniston
    D. David Schwimmer

33. What sci-fi TV-series is called "Aux Frontières Du Reel" in France?

    A. *Star Trek: Voyager*
    B. *The X-Files*
    C. *The Twilight Zone*
    D. *The Outer Limits*

34. Who played Charles in the '80s show *Charles in Charge*?

    A. Kirk Cameron
    B. Michael J.Fox
    C. Scott Baio
    D. Joey Lawrence

35. What is Sylvester Stallone's real first name?

    A. Michael
    B. Anthony
    C. Timothy
    D. Matthew

36. Who was the first African-American to win the Best
    New Artist Grammy Award in 1975?

    A. Diana Ross
    B. Natalie Cole
    C. Michael Jackson
    D. Stevie Wonder

37. A contestant who freezes in front of the camera on
    a game show is usually called what?

    A. Ice man
    B. Scarecrow
    C. Bambi
    D. Space case

38. Which of these artists did *not* endorse the Coca-Cola
    company?

    A. Guess Who
    B. The Drifters
    C. The Beach Boys
    D. The Beatles

39. What rap singer made his television debut in an ad-
    vertisement for Baskin-Robbins?

    A. Sean "Puffy" Combs
    B. Coolio
    C. Master P
    D. M. C. Hammer

40. Before Christian Slater took over, what young actor was originally slated to play the role of the interviewer in the 1994 film *Interview With the Vampire*?

    A. Johnny Depp
    B. Stephen Dorff
    C. Keanu Reeves
    D. River Phoenix

41. What Beatle was reported to be dead by the tabloid *The Northern Star* on September 26, 1969?

    A. Paul McCartney
    B. Ringo Starr
    C. John Lennon
    D. George Harrison

42. Carly Simon's hit "You're So Vain" was rumored to have been written about what actor?

    A. Jack Nicholson
    B. Warren Beatty
    C. Robert Redford
    D. Paul Newman

43. How many films did the dance duo Ginger Rogers and Fred Astaire make together?

    A. 3
    B. 6
    C. 10
    D. 14

44. What Jack Nicholson film was retitled as *Mr. Cat Poop* in China?

    A. *Terms of Endearment*
    B. *Chinatown*
    C. *One Flew Over the Cuckoo's Nest*
    D. *As Good as it Gets*

45. What was the last song played by the Beatles during their last concert at Candlestick Park?

    A. "Long Tall Sally"
    B. "Eleanor Rigby"
    C. "Yellow Brick Road"
    D. "Hey Bulldog"

46. What was the first CD made for commercial distribution in America?

    A. Michael Jackson's *Thriller*
    B. Madonna's *Like a Virgin*
    C. Bruce Springstein's *Born in the USA*
    D. U2's *The Joshua Tree*

47. Who was the first television sitcom couple to share the same bed on the air?

    A. June and Ward Cleaver
    B. Carol and Mike Brady
    C. Lucy and Desi Arnaz
    D. Lily and Herman Munster

48. What was the first soap opera to win an Emmy award in 1972?

    A. *The Doctors*
    B. *General Hospital*
    C. *All my Children*
    D. *Another World*

49. What 1994 action film starring Arnold Schwarze-negger was protested by the American-Arab Anti-Discrimination Committee at a Washington theater?

   A. *True Lies*
   B. *Total Recall*
   C. *Terminator II*
   D. *Eraser*

50. What TV sitcom was the first to film an episode in Moscow?

   A. *Mork & Mindy*
   B. *Head of the Class*
   C. *Bosom Buddies*
   D. *All in the Family*

51. During the making of the *Wizard of Oz*, the "little people" earned $50 a week. How much did Toto earn per week?

   A. $50
   B. $75
   C. $100
   D. $125

52. Who was the only cast member on *M*A*S*H* to serve in the Korean War?

   A. Alan Alda
   B. Jamie Farr
   C. Harry Morgan
   D. McLean Stevenson

53. Who was the first and only actress to receive a Golden Globe Award for "Most Glamorous Actress" in 1959?

   A. Sophia Loren
   B. Marilyn Monroe
   C. Zsa Zsa Gabor
   D. Ann Margaret

54. Which of these actors did not play the "The Saint" in film or television?

   A. George Sanders
   B. Rutger Hauer
   C. Roger Moore
   D. Val Kilmer

55. Who was the first stand-up comedian Johnny Carson ever invited to sit on *The Tonight Show* couch during their first guest appearance?

   A. Jerry Seinfeld
   B. Brett Butler
   C. Dennis Miller
   D. Ellen DeGeneres

56. How many weeks did Elvis Presley's hit single "Love Me Tender" stay on the Billboard charts?

   A. 6
   B. 12
   C. 19
   D. 28

57. Aerosmith's "Dude Looks Like a Lady" was written about what glam rocker?

A. Prince
B. Mick Jagger
C. David Bowie
D. Vince Neil

58. What model turned actress starred in the 1984 film *Greystoke: The Legend of Tarzan, Lord of the Apes*?

A. Andie McDowell
B. Elle Macpherson
C. Sharon Stone
D. Kelly LeBrock

59. Who was the first Beatle to have a No. 1 hit with the single "My Sweet Lord" after the group's breakup?

A. Paul McCartney
B. John Lennon
C. George Harrison
D. Ringo Starr

60. What silent-film starlet made a dramatic turn in Billy Wilder's *Sunset Boulevard* when she was 52 years old?

A. Dorothy Cumming
B. Gloria Swanson
C. Edith Yorke
D. Dorothy Revier

61. Which of the following is not one of the Marx brothers?

    A. Groucho
    B. Rico
    C. Harpo
    D. Zeppo

62. In what 1984 film did Dolly Parton and Sylvester Stallone make a not-so-winning combination?

    A. *Romancing the Stone*
    B. *Rhinestone*
    C. *Bird on a Wire*
    D. *Oscar*

63. What actor has *not* portrayed Wild West dentist Doc Holliday in film?

    A. Dennis Quaid
    B. Kirk Douglas
    C. Michael J. Fox
    D. Val Kilmer

64. What Demi Moore 1996 film bombed domestically, but went on to earn $70 million outside of the United States?

    A. *G.I. Jane*
    B. *Striptease*
    C. *Indecent Proposal*
    D. *The Butcher's Wife*

65. What is the name of the camel on the Camel cigarettes pack?

   A. Old Joe
   B. Old Bob
   C. Old Tom
   D. Old Ed

66. What *Magnum P.I.* hunk made two appearances on the *Dating Game* without ever being picked?

   A. Roger E. Mosley
   B. Tom Selleck
   C. John Hillerman
   D. Larry Manetti

67. What late-night talk show host has a fondness for riding Harley-Davidson motorcycles?

   A. David Letterman
   B. Jay Leno
   C. Conan O'Brien
   D. Bill Mahr

68. What actor said, "Frankly, my dear, I don't give a damn" in *Gone with the Wind*?

   A. Clark Gable
   B. John Barrymore
   C. Spencer Tracy
   D. Humphrey Bogart

69. What famous French actress was recognized for her contribution to animal rights?

   A. Jeanne Moreau
   B. Juliette Binoche
   C. Catherine Deneuve
   D. Brigitte Bardot

70. In what film did Jim Carrey say, "If I'm not back in five minutes, wait longer"?

    A. *The Mask*
    B. *Ace Ventura: Pet Detective*
    C. *Dumb and Dumber*
    D. *Ace Ventura: When Nature Calls*

71. What comedian said, "I'm not afraid to die. I just don't want to be there when it happens."

    A. Woody Allen
    B. Lenny Bruce
    C. Jerry Seinfeld
    D. Andy Rooney

72. What was the single-letter name of James Bond's gadget man?

    A. T
    B. Q
    C. P
    D. X

73. What company was responsible for the most expensive commercial ever made, with a price tag of $600,000 to $1 million?

    A. Nike
    B. McDonald's
    C. Apple
    D. Pepsi

74. What cartoonist created "Fritz the Cat"?

    A. Jim Davis
    B. Charles M. Schultz
    C. Pat Sullivan
    D. Hank Ketchum

75. Which of the following was *not* one of Donald Duck's nephews?

   A. Huey
   B. Ronny
   C. Dewey
   D. Louie

76. In Disney's *The Lion King,* what is the name of Simba's father?

   A. Mufasa
   B. Mephisto
   C. Mustafa
   D. Mastifo

77. On Valentine's Day of 1999, Goth singer Marylin Manson asked which actress to marry him?

   A. Christina Ricci
   B. Rose McGowen
   C. Claire Danes
   D. Jennifer Love Hewitt

78. What nationality are the inventors of the game "Trivial Pursuit"?

   A. French
   B. American
   C. Canadian
   D. British

79. What was the first video to air on MTV?

   A. The Buggles' "Video Killed the Radio Star"
   B. Pat Benatar's "Love is a Battlefield"
   C. Michael Jackson's "Billie Jean"
   D. Rod Stewart's "Do Ya Think I'm Sexy"

80. Which of the following actors played James Bond only once?

    A. Sean Connery
    B. Timothy Dalton
    C. David Niven
    D. Pierce Brosnan

81. 714 Evergreen Terrace, Springfield, is the address of what television family?

    A. The Bunkers
    B. The Cosbys
    C. The Simpsons
    D. The Salingers

82. Who was the only person to appear on *TV Guide* three weeks in a row?

    A. Jerry Seinfeld
    B. George Clooney
    C. Ted Danson
    D. Michael Landon

83. Which of the following TV shows is not a spinoff?

    A. *All in the Family*
    B. *Angel*
    C. *Cheers*
    D. *The Jeffersons*

84. What was the name of the airplane in which Buddy Holly died?

    A. *The Eagle*
    B. *American Pie*
    C. *Serenity*
    D. *Commander*

85. What actress depicted country music star Loretta Lynn in the film *Coal Miner's Daughter*?

A. Sally Field
B. Dolly Parton
C. Sissy Spacek
D. Jane Fonda

86. Which of the following films was not directed by Stanley Kubrick?

A. *Alien*
B. *Eyes Wide Shut*
C. *Spartacus*
D. *2001: A Space Odyssey*

87. Larry Flynt is the publisher of what adult magazine?

A. *Playboy*
B. *Hustler*
C. *Penthouse*
D. *Playgirl*

88. Veronica and Betty were the girlfriends of what comic book hero?

A. Dave
B. Calvin
C. Dilbert
D. Archie

89. REM's song "Man on the Moon" is about which comedian?

A. Lenny Bruce
B. Steven Wright
C. Danny Devito
D. Andy Kaufman

90. Which of the following was not one of The Monkees?

    A. Micky Dolenz
    B. David Cassidy
    C. Peter Tork
    D. Davy Jones

91. What '80s singing sensation made a cameo appearance in the 1992 film *Boomerang*?

    A. Diana Ross
    B. Cyndi Lauper
    C. Cher
    D. Grace Jones

92. What was the name of the first Barbie doll sold in 1959?

    A. Barbie Teenage Fashion Model
    B. Glamour Barbie
    C. Dress Me Up Barbie
    D. Hollywood Barbie

93. Which of the following was *not* one of the seven dwarfs in *Snow White and the Seven Dwarfs*?

    A. Sleepy
    B. Grouchy
    C. Bashful
    D. Dopey

94. What is the name of Superman's girlfriend?

    A. Wonder Woman
    B. Lois Lane
    C. Vicky Vale
    D. Polly Purebread

95. Ruth, Bonnie, Anita, and June are otherwise known as what musical group?

   A. The Supremes
   B. The Bangles
   C. The Rondells
   D. The Pointer Sisters

96. The LP *Emotional Rescue* was recorded by what musical group in 1980?

   A. The Rolling Stones
   B. The Who
   C. The Cars
   D. The Replacements

97. Billy Joel was born in what part of New York?

   A. Long Island
   B. Brooklyn
   C. Staten Island
   D. Buffalo

98. Bill Haley and the Comets were responsible for what popular tune in the 1950s?

   A. "Earth Angel"
   B. "Rock around the Clock"
   C. "Why do Fools Fall in Love"
   D. "Tutti Frutti"

99. Tom and Jerry were the early pseudonyms of which famous singing duo?

   A. Sonny and Cher
   B. The Captain and Tennille
   C. The Carpenters
   D. Simon and Garfunkle

100. Of the following movies, which did Bill Conti *not* write the score for?

    A. *The Karate Kid*
    B. *Gotcha!*
    C. *Terms of Endearment*
    D. *Lean of Me*

101. What famous singer/songwriter penned the theme song for *The Monkees* television show?

    A. Tom Jones
    B. Neil Diamond
    C. Barry Manillow .
    D. Burt Bacharach

102. What Latin heartthrob's real last name is Morales?

    A. Enrique Iglesias
    B. Marc Anthony
    C. Luis Miguel
    D. Ricky Martin

103. What actress portrayed the "prom queen" in John Hughes's classic teen flick *The Breakfast Club*?

    A. Ally Sheedy
    B. Heather Locklear
    C. Molly Ringwald
    D. Lea Thompson

104. What actor's bowler and cane were sold at Christies' in London for £82,500?

    A. Fred Astaire
    B. James Cagney
    C. Fred Sinatra
    D. Charlie Chaplin

105. Who was the first British rocker to perform in the USSR in 1979?

    A. Paul McCartney
    B. David Bowie
    C. Elton John
    D. Eric Clapton

106. What popular board game did Charles Darrow invent in 1934?

    A. Scrabble
    B. Boggle
    C. Trivial Pursuit
    D. Monopoly

107. What author first introduced James Bond in the book *Casino Royale*?

    A. Colin Dexter
    B. Ian Fleming
    C. Elmore Leonard
    D. James Cain

108. What was the first video game ever to be invented?

    A. Tetris
    B. Centipede
    C. Spacewar
    D. Pong

109. What was the first group to go platinum, with a million copies sold of their *Greatest Hits* LP in 1976?

    A. The Rolling Stones
    B. Fleetwood Mac
    C. The Eagles
    D. The Beatles

110. What female group recorded the 1940s hit "Boogie Woogie Bugle Boy"?

    A. The Supremes
    B. The Andrews Sisters
    C. The Rondells
    D. The Coyote Sisters

111. What popular TV personality starred in CBS's *Who Do You Trust?* in 1956?

    A. Johnny Carson
    B. Ed McMahon
    C. Dick Clark
    D. Andy Rooney

112. Whom did Bryant Gumble replace as co-host of NBC's *The Today Show* in 1982?

    A. Peter Jennings
    B. Chris Wallace
    C. Tom Brokaw
    D. Hugh Downs

113. How many of Stephen King's books have been adapted for the big screen?

    A. 8
    B. 16
    C. 27
    D. 34

114. Which of the following is *not* a Madonna album?

    A. *Like a Virgin*
    B. *Like a Prayer*
    C. *Truth or Dare*
    D. *True Blue*

115. Which of the following movies is not an Adam Sandler vehicle?

    A. *Dumb and Dumber*
    B. *Billy Madison*
    C. *Big Daddy*
    D. *The Waterboy*

116. Who was the youngest host on *Saturday Night Live*?

    A. Christina Ricci
    B. Drew Barrymore
    C. Macauly Culkin
    D. Tatum O'Neal

117. How much did it cost to make James Cameron's *Titanic*?

    A. $100 million
    B. $200 million
    C. $300 million
    D. $1 billion

118. Who has never been a "lady of the WB"?

    A. Shannon Doherty
    B. Tori Spelling
    C. Sarah Michelle Gellar
    D. Keri Russel

119. Which movie did *not* feature Robert DeNiro?

    A. *The Godfather*
    B. *Taxi Driver*
    C. *Awakenings*
    D. *Once Upon a Time in America*

120. Which of these movie-related inventions came first?

   A. Drive-in theater
   B. Talking films
   C. Nude star
   D. DVD

CHAPTER FIVE

HISTORY AND POLITICS

1. What was the official language in England for over 600 years?

   A. Italian
   B. Latin
   C. French
   D. Spanish

2. Who was the serial killer responsible for the brutal murder of director Roman Polanski's wife Sharon Tate?

   A. Charles Manson
   B. John Wayne Gacy
   C. Ted Bundy
   D. Richard Speck

3. Where was Malcolm X born?

   A. Memphis, Tennessee
   B. Omaha, Nebraska
   C. Lansing, Michigan
   D. Kansas City, Kansas

4. What is the symbol of the U.S. Republican Party?

   A. Donkey
   B. Elephant
   C. Bear
   D. Bull

5. Which of these four presidents' faces is *not* carved on Mt. Rushmore?

   A. George Washington
   B. Thomas Jefferson
   C. Andrew Jackson
   D. Teddy Roosevelt

6. Who was the first President born in the twentieth century?

   A. Jimmy Carter
   B. John F. Kennedy
   C. Richard Nixon
   D. Dwight Eisenhower

7. What was the first country to legalize abortion in 1920?

   A. Russia
   B. United States
   C. France
   D. China

8. What was the name of the first space shuttle before President Ford changed it to the *Enterprise* after receiving 100,000 letters from *Star Trek* fans?

   A. *Endurance*
   B. *Survivor*
   C. *Challenger*
   D. *The Constitution*

9. Where did the Battle of Bunker Hill take place?

   A. Plymouth Rock
   B. Bunker Hill
   C. Breed's Hill
   D. Chapel Hill

10. What year did the U.S. enter WWII?

   A. 1939
   B. 1941
   C. 1943
   D. 1945

11. What President's administration is the shortest in U.S. history?

   A. James Garfield
   B. Andrew Johnson
   C. Gerald Ford
   D. William Henry Harrison

12. Who was the first President to be sworn into office by a woman?

   A. Lyndon Johnson
   B. Herbert Hoover
   C. John F. Kennedy
   D. Calvin Coolidge

13. What President ran for office unopposed?

   A. John Adams
   B. James Monroe
   C. Ulysses S. Grant
   D. Zachary Taylor

14. Who was the oldest President upon leaving office?

   A. Theodore Roosevelt
   B. Abraham Lincoln
   C. Ronald Reagan
   D. Andrew Johnson

15. Who was the only President never to get married?

   A. James Buchanan
   B. Dwight Eisenhower
   C. Warren Harding
   D. James Madison

16. Who was the first President to leave office prior to his term expiring for reasons other than death?

   A. Richard Nixon
   B. John Adams
   C. Andrew Johnson
   D. Abraham Lincoln

17. In what century did Christmas become a U.S. national holiday?

   A. 17th
   B. 18th
   C. 19th
   D. 20th

18. Who was the first and only President to win non-consecutive terms to the White House?

   A. Grover Cleveland
   B. Andrew Jackson
   C. Thomas Jefferson
   D. George Washington

19. Which President created the Order of the Purple Heart to commemorate enlisted officers?

   A. George Washington
   B. Theodore Roosevelt
   C. Warren Harding
   D. John F. Kennedy

20. What was the first country to abolish capital punishment in 1787?

    A. Thailand
    B. Switzerland
    C. Finland
    D. Austria

21. The White House was originally painted what color before switching to white after the war of 1812?

    A. Yellow
    B. Red
    C. Blue
    D. Gray

22. In what city was the Liberty Bell made?

    A. Philadelphia
    B. London
    C. Paris
    D. Boston

23. Which is the only U.S. state that has been under six flags, including the flags of Spain, France, and Mexico?

    A. Hawaii
    B. Alaska
    C. Arizona
    D. Texas

24. Which of the thirteen original colonies was the first to declare independence from England?

    A. New Hampshire
    B. Massachusetts
    C. Rhode Island
    D. Maryland

25. The Boston Tea Party of 1773 was the result of what tax imposed on tea?

   A. 1 cent per pound
   B. 3 cents per pound
   C. 6 cents per pound
   D. 9 cents per pound

26. Who is the only man whose birthday is a legal holiday in every U.S. state?

   A. Abraham Lincoln
   B. George Washington
   C. Martin Luther King Jr.
   D. Christopher Columbus

27. Which holiday were Eastern Europeans permitted to celebrate openly for the first time in 1989?

   A. Easter
   B. Hanukkah
   C. Christmas
   D. Passover

28. What coin was first minted in the U.S. on October 15, 1974?

   A. Silver dollar
   B. Half-dollar
   C. Quarter
   D. Penny

29. What is the minimum age set for the President by the Constitution?

   A. 25
   B. 35
   C. 45
   D. 55

30. Who was the youngest person to take on the role of President at 42 years of age?

    A. Theodore Roosevelt
    B. John F. Kennedy
    C. Warren Harding
    D. Woodrow Wilson

31. Of all the United States Presidents, who was the shortest, measuring at 5 feet, 4 inches tall?

    A. Abraham Lincoln
    B. Ronald Reagan
    C. James Madison
    D. George Bush

32. Who was the only son of a President to serve as President himself?

    A. John Quincy Adams
    B. Andrew Johnson
    C. James Garfield
    D. Benjamin Harrison

33. Which French ruler was nicknamed the "Sun King" during his reign from 1643–1715?

    A. Napoleon Bonaparte
    B. Louis-Philippe I
    C. Louis X
    D. Louis XIV

34. Which dictator was voted "man of the year" by *Time* magazine in 1938?

    A. Joseph Stalin
    B. Adolf Hitler
    C. Francisco Franco
    D. Benito Mussolini

35. Where was Napoleon Bonaparte born?

    A. Spain
    B. France
    C. Germany
    D. Italy

36. Which country gave the U.S. the Statue of Liberty?

    A. England
    B. Sweden
    C. France
    D. Italy

37. Which President served the shortest term in office,
    after falling ill with pneumonia shortly after the in-
    auguration?

    A. Benjamin Harrison
    B. Andrew Jackson
    C. William Harrison
    D. Franklin Pierce

38. What was the color of American uniforms worn by
    soldiers during the Revolutionary War?

    A. Red
    B. Green
    C. Purple
    D. Blue

39. Which famous American's picture did Adolph Hitler
    keep framed on his desk?

    A. Thomas Edison
    B. Ulysses S. Grant
    C. Henry Ford
    D. Benjamin Franklin

40. Which President authored the book *No More Vietnams*?

    A. Richard Nixon
    B. Lyndon Johnson
    C. George Bush
    D. Jimmy Carter

41. Who was the first President to win a Noble Peace Prize?

    A. Theodore Roosevelt
    B. Gerald Ford
    C. Thomas Jefferson
    D. James Polk

42. John F. Kennedy was responsible for establishing which philanthropic organization during his term in office?

    A. Greenpeace
    B. The Peace Corps
    C. PETA
    D. Habitat for Humanity

43. What famous speech was given on November 19, 1863?

    A. "Day of Infamy" Address
    B. Gettysburg Address
    C. Checkers Speech
    D. Lincoln's Thanksgiving Proclamation

44. Which U.S. President demanded a "return to normalcy"?

    A. Harry S. Truman
    B. Grover Cleveland
    C. Warren G. Harding
    D. John F. Kennedy

45. To whom was First Lady Mary Ann Todd married to?

    A. George Washington
    B. Abraham Lincoln
    C. Andrew Jackson
    D. William Taft

46. Franklin D. Roosevelt held office in which political position before becoming President?

    A. Governor
    B. Senator
    C. Mayor
    D. Congressman

47. Who was the first African-American woman in space?

    A. Shannon Lucid
    B. Mae Jemison
    C. Roberta Bondar
    D. Valentina Tereshkova

48. The famous gunfight at the O.K. Corral took place in what city?

    A. Lincoln, Nebraska
    B. Tombstone, Arizona
    C. El Paso, Texas
    D. Santa Fe, New Mexico

49. Who was the twelfth President of the United States?

    A. Zachary Taylor
    B. James Polk
    C. John Tyler
    D. Millard Fillmore

50. Who was the first woman justice to be admitted into the Supreme Court?

    A. Ruth Bader Ginsburg
    B. Sarah Weddington
    C. Sandra Day O'Conner
    D. Janet Reno

51. The development of the A-bomb was classified under what code name?

    A. Operation 000
    B. Mission Space Probe
    C. Liberty Project
    D. Manhattan Project

52. In 1912, the *Carpathia* answered a signal from what sinking ship?

    A. *Victoria*
    B. *Atlantis*
    C. *Titanic*
    D. *Queen Mary*

53. What scandal rocked the nation, earning the *Washinton Post* a Pulitzer Prize in 1973?

    A. Whitewater
    B. Watergate
    C. Iran Contra Affair
    D. S & L Scandal

54. During what demonstration did Martin Luther King Jr. deliver his famous "I Have a Dream Speech"?

    A. Million Man March
    B. Montgomery Bus Boycott
    C. March on Washington
    D. Birmingham March

55. Which holiday honors the defeat of Napoleon III's army in 1862?

    A. Cinco De Mayo
    B. Mardi Gras
    C. Ramadan
    D. Dia de los Muertos

56. What Native American was referred to as "The Red Napoleon" by the press in 1877?

    A. Sitting Bull
    B. Chief Joseph
    C. Hiawatha
    D. Red Jacket

57. What established the precedence allowing the United States to expand westward?

    A. The Yorktown Campaign
    B. The Townshend Acts
    C. The Northwest Ordinance
    D. The Louisiana Purchase

58. What news anchor worked as a press aid for Richard Nixon?

    A. Connie Chung
    B. Diane Sawyer
    C. Barbara Walters
    D. Debra Norville

59. Tibet was taken over by which communist nation in 1950?

   A. Soviet Union
   B. China
   C. Czechoslovakia
   D. Poland

60. What philosopher and economist wrote the *Communist Manifesto* in 1848?

   A. David Hume
   B. John Stuart Mill
   C. Karl Marx
   D. Ludwig Von Mises

61. Alexis de Tocqueville was responsible for writing which famous treatise?

   A. *Democracy in America*
   B. *Common Sense*
   C. *On Liberty*
   D. *Birds of America*

62. What ship safely transported the Pilgrims to Plymouth Rock?

   A. The *Dona Paz*
   B. The *Estonia*
   C. The *Mayflower*
   D. The *Normandie*

63. Which of the following is not one of the seven wonders of the world?

   A. The Great Pyramid of Giza
   B. The Colossus of Alexandria
   C. The Statue of Zeus at Olympia
   D. The Mausoleum at Halicarnassus

64. Which war, lasting from to 1337 to 1453, resolved a conflict between France and England?

    A. The Hundred Years War
    B. Boer Wars
    C. Punic Wars
    D. Napoleanic Wars

65. Which Civil War battle gave Abraham Lincoln the victory needed to pass the Emancipation Proclamation?

    A. Battle of Shiloh
    B. Battle of Antietam
    C. Battle of Vicksburg
    D. Battle of Fort Sumter

66. The Bolsheviks and Mensheviks were two rival political factions from which country?

    A. Turkey
    B. Romania
    C. Germany
    D. Russia

67. Which plague killed millions of people throughout Europe during the Dark Ages?

    A. Bubonic Plague
    B. The Typhoid Plague
    C. The Yellow Fever
    D. The Red Menace

68. The Constitution requires how many jurors in a Federal court case?

    A. 8
    B. 10
    C. 12
    D. 14

69. Which mad Roman emperor ordered his troops to collect seashells as "spoils of the sea"?

    A. Claudius
    B. Caligula
    C. Galerius
    D. Tiberius

70. Who made the famous solo flight across the Atlantic in 1927?

    A. Rene Fonck
    B. John Alcock
    C. Arthur Brown
    D. Charles Lindbergh

71. Who replaced Neville Chamberlain as prime minister of England in 1940?

    A. Tony Blair
    B. Winston Churchill
    C. Margaret Thatcher
    D. James Callaghan

72. Which of the following was *not* one of Lenin's pseudonyms?

    A. Pertov
    B. Tulin
    C. Sergei
    D. Ivanov

73. Which Chinese leader proclaimed the People's Republic of China as Chiang Kai-shek in 1949?

    A. Sun Yat-sen
    B. Mao Zedong
    C. Chiang Kai-shek
    D. Hua Guofeng

74. Who was the president of Russia from 1985 to 1991?

    A. Boris Yeltsin
    B. Mikhail Gorbachev
    C. Nikita Khrushchev
    D. Yuri Andropov

75. In what year did Pope John Paul II and Mikhail Gorbachev end a 70-year cold war between the Roman Catholic Church and the Soviet Union?

    A. 1986
    B. 1987
    C. 1988
    D. 1989

76. The 1729 Treaty of Seville was signed by all of the following countries except . . .

    A. Spain
    B. Italy
    C. France
    D. England

77. In what year did Frederick the Great become the king of Prussia?

    A. 1720
    B. 1730
    C. 1740
    D. 1750

78. Which explorer discovered Alaska and the Aleutian Islands only to die shortly after from hunger and exposure?

    A. Victor Behring
    B. Marco Polo
    C. Sebastian Cabot
    D. Wifred Thesiger

79. What famous war marked a conflict between England and France and lasted from 1756–63?

    A. Punic War
    B. Seven Years' War
    C. Crimean War
    D. Norman Conquest

80. Which act was passed in 1765 that would allow the U.S. colonies to be taxed?

    A. The Townshend Acts
    B. The Coercive Acts
    C. The Stamp Act
    D. The Sugar Acts

81. In what year did the "Boston Massacre" take place?

    A. 1770
    B. 1780
    C. 1790
    D. 1800

82. How many mercenaries did England hire to fight during the American Revolution?

    A. 5,000
    B. 16,000
    C. 29,000
    D. 35,000

83. How many U.S. colonies signed the Declaration of Independence in 1776?

    A. 10
    B. 11
    C. 12
    D. 13

84. The signing of which treaty ended the American Revolution?

    A. Treaty of Paris
    B. Treaty of Geenville
    C. Treaty of Grenada
    D. Treaty of Sèvres

85. In what country did a mob storm the Bastille?

    A. Italy
    B. Spain
    C. France
    D. Germany

86. In what year was the Constitution of the United States signed?

    A. 1787
    B. 1788
    C. 1789
    D. 1790

87. In what year was Prohibition repealed in the United
    States?

    A. 1923
    B. 1927
    C. 1933
    D. 1936

88. A nuclear reactor exploded in what Eastern European city in 1986?

    A. Lodz, Poland
    B. Tbilisi, USSR
    C. Chernobyl, USSR
    D. Kazan, USSR

89. Which famous war hero is known as "King of the
    Wild Frontier"?

    A. Crispus Attucks
    B. Davy Crockett
    C. William Barret Travis
    D. Robert E. Lee

90. Who was the first British monarch to live in Buckingham Palace?

    A. Queen Elizabeth
    B. Queen Victoria
    C. Queen Mary
    D. Queen Mary II

91. In what state was the American flag first raised on
    land in 1776?

    A. Massachusetts
    B. New York
    C. Rhode Island
    D. Delaware

92. Which President signed the Emancipation Proclamation?

    A. James Garfield
    B. Abraham Lincoln
    C. Zachary Taylor
    D. George Washington

93. Where was the immigrant handling depot located in New York?

    A. Battery Park
    B. Ellis Island
    C. Staten Island
    D. Long Island

94. Which of these political figures was *not* found guilty of conspiracy to obstruct the Watergate investigation?

    A. Attorney General John Mitchell
    B. H. R. Haldeman
    C. John Ehrlichman
    D. President Richard Nixon

95. Where was former CNN foreign correspondent Arthur Kent stationed when he earned his nickname "the Scud Stud"?

    A. Kosovo
    B. The Persian Gulf
    C. Granada
    D. Boznia-Herzegovina

96. Which decade saw segregation get banned from the army by executive order?

   A. 1950s
   B. 1960s
   C. 1940s
   D. 1930s

97. Which was the only nation that refused to sign the Geneva Accords at the 1954 Geneva Conference on Vietnam?

   A. The Soviet Union
   B. The United States
   C. China
   D. France

98. How many students were killed at the Kent State massacre on May 4, 1970?

   A. 4
   B. 8
   C. 12
   D. 16

99. Whose presidency was marred by the Teapot Dome scandal?

   A. Franklin Delano Roosevelt
   B. Herbert Hoover
   C. Warren Harding
   D. Woodrow Wilson

100. During the Great Depression, what did people dub the newspapers that the homeless used as makeshift blankets?

   A. Cold covers
   B. Hobo blankets
   C. Yesterday's news
   D. Hoover blankets

101. What was the name of Russia's St. Petersburg before the Soviet Union disbanded?

   A. Stalingrad
   B. Petrograd
   C. Leningrad
   D. Volgograd

102. Which battle finally brought an end to Napoleon's empire?

   A. Austerlitz
   B. Elba
   C. Waterloo
   D. Borodino

103. Who led France's Reign of Terror?

   A. Robespierre
   B. Napoleon
   C. Marie Antoinette
   D. Marat

104. Who came first?

   A. Attila the Hun
   B. Alexander the Great
   C. Charlemagne
   D. Genghis Khan

105. In what year did the Louisiana Purchase take place?

    A. 1789
    B. 1803
    C. 1811
    D. 1817

106. Which leader is portrayed on the cover of the book *The Day of the Jackal*?

    A. Charles De Gaulle
    B. Fidel Castro
    C. Winston Churchill
    D. Joseph Stalin

107. "The Prince of Sorrows" was the nickname for which British monarch?

    A. Prince Edward
    B. Prince Charles
    C. Prince Philip
    D. Prince Andrew

108. In what year did Rudolph Giuliani put Ivan Boesky in jail?

    A. 1985
    B. 1986
    C. 1987
    D. 1988

109. What fashion icon designed uniforms for the Italian air force?

    A. Paola Frani
    B. Georgio Armani
    C. Romeo Gigli
    D. Angela Missoni

110. What human rights leader was sentenced to life imprisonment in 1964?

    A. Nelson Mandela
    B. Huda Shaarawi
    C. Malcolm X
    D. Oscar Romero

111. How many times was Mikhail Gorbachev *Time* magazine's Man of the Year?

    A. 0
    B. 1
    C. 2
    D. 3

112. What invention altered the postal business in 1839?

    A. Stamps
    B. Ink
    C. Zip codes
    D. Envelopes

113. What space shuttle was the *Challenger* replaced by?

    A. *Atlantic*
    B. *Discovery*
    C. *Columbia*
    D. *Voyager*

114. How much did the stock market drop in value during Black Monday on October 19, 1987?

    A. 13%
    B. 18%
    C. 22%
    D. 25%

115. Where did the 1989 summit meeting between President Bush and Mikhail Gorbachev take place?

    A. Russia
    B. United States
    C. Latvia
    D. Malta

116. What was the only country to register zero births in 1983?

    A. Lichtenstein
    B. Netherlands
    C. Monaco
    D. Vatican City

117. The Leaning Tower of Pisa is leaning in what direction?

    A. North
    B. South
    C. East
    D. West

118. A total of how many men have walked on the moon?

    A. 6
    B. 12
    C. 18
    D. 24

119. In what year did Britain introduce the very first income tax?

    A. 1787
    B. 1788
    C. 1789
    D. 1790

120. While at Harvard University, Edward Kennedy was
     suspended for cheating on what exam?

     A. English
     B. History
     C. Spanish
     D. Economics

CHAPTER SIX

ART AND LITERATURE

1. What is the oldest letter in the alphabet?

    A. A
    B. P
    C. O
    D. Z

2. What is the longest-running show on Broadway?

    A. *Phantom of the Opera*
    B. *A Chorus Line*
    C. *Cats*
    D. *Showboat*

3. What is the longest-running play in history?

    A. Tennessee Williams's *A Streetcar Named Desire*
    B. Arthur Miller's *Death of a Salesman*
    C. Agatha Christie's *The Mouse Trap*
    D. Oscar Wilde's *The Importance of Being Earnest*

4. In which Shakespearean play did a ghost *not* make an appearance?

    A. *Othello*
    B. *Julius Caesar*
    C. *Richard III*
    D. *Hamlet*

5. Which of these novels is not set in England?

   A. Edith Wharton's *Age of Innocence*
   B. Emily Bronte's *Wuthering Heights*
   C. Jane Austen's *Pride and Prejudice*
   D. Oscar Wilde's *The Portrait of Dorian Gray*

6. The author of *Portrait of a Lady* also wrote . . . ?

   A. *Northanger Abbey*
   B. *The Awakening*
   C. *Turn of the Screw*
   D. *The Shining*

7. Which composer is responsible for "The Flight of the Bumble Bee"?

   A. Nikolai Rimsky-Korsakov
   B. Sergei Rachmaninoff
   C. Ludwig Van Beethoven
   D. Igor Fyodorovich Stravinsky

8. The statue "The Thinker" by Auguste Rodin was intended to represent which poet?

   A. Dante
   B. Lord Byron
   C. John Milton
   D. Paul Valery

9. According to Greek mythology, who was the goddess of rainbows?

   A. Athena
   B. Aphrodite
   C. Iris
   D. Venus

10. What Russian novelist wrote *Lolita*?

   A. Marcus Levitt
   B. Anton Checkov
   C. Vladimir Nabokov
   D. Fedorov Vasilii

11. Artist Andy Warhol became famous for painting cans of what?

   A. Tuna
   B. Vegetables
   C. Soup
   D. Meats

12. What artist is considered to be the leading landscape painter in the world?

   A. Claude Monet
   B. Auguste Rodin
   C. Camille Pissaro
   D. Casper David Freidrich

13. Which of the following painters gave the world "The Mona Lisa"?

   A. Peter Paul Rubens
   B. Michelangelo
   C. Leonardo da Vinci
   D. Nicolas Poussin

14. Which of the following is *not* a fairy tale written by Hans Christian Anderson?

   A. *The Ugly Duckling*
   B. *The Snow Queen*
   C. *The Pine Tree*
   D. *Cinderella*

15. What French writer wrote *The Red and the Black*?

    A. Gustave Flaubert
    B. Emile Zola
    C. Honore Balzac
    D. Renate Stendhal

16. Who said, "Consistency is the last resort of the unimaginative"?

    A. Oscar Wilde
    B. T. S. Elliot
    C. Henry David Thoreau
    D. Ralph Waldo Emerson

17. What French philosopher spouted, "Hell is other people"?

    A. Albert Camus
    B. Jean-Paul Sartre
    C. Jean Jacques Rousseau
    D. Blaise Pascal

18. According to Greek mythology, who is the god of the sea?

    A. Apollo
    B. Zeus
    C. Hades
    D. Poseidon

19. Where did Diana's daughter, Persephone, have to spend half the year?

    A. Enchanted Forest
    B. The Temple of Delphi
    C. The Underworld
    D. King Midas' Palace

20. From which author's novel did the band Steppen-wolf, formerly known as "The Sparrows," borrow their name?

A. E. M. Forester
B. Richard Yates
C. Herman Hesse
D. Truman Capote

21. Steely Dan borrowed their name from a sexual de-vice featured in what William Burroughs' novel?

A. *Naked Lunch*
B. *Junky*
C. *The Soft Machine*
D. *Exterminator*

22. After the Bible, what is the most translated book in the world?

A. Dr. Seuss's *Green Eggs and Ham*
B. J. D. Salinger's *The Catcher in the Rye*
C. Cervantes's *Don Quixote*
D. Leo Tolstoy's *War and Peace*

23. What is the bestselling children's book of all time?

A. *Curious George*
B. *Winnie the Pooh*
C. *Alice in Wonderland*
D. *The Tales of Peter Rabbit*

24. Which legendary musician was nicknamed "Satch-mo"?

A. Miles Davis
B. John Coltrane
C. Louis Armstrong
D. Nat King Cole

25. Who wrote *The Canterbury Tales*?

    A. Geoffrey Chaucer
    B. Edmund Spenser
    C. Sir Thomas More
    D. William Shakespeare

26. Who composed the music for *Wizard of Oz*?

    A. Jerome Kern
    B. Harold Arlen
    C. Ira Gershwin
    D. Andrew Lloyd Weber

27. Which of the following novels was *not* written by French author Guy de Maupassant?

    A. *A Life*
    B. *Père Goriot*
    C. *Bel-Ami*
    D. *Pierre et Jean*

28. What Russian author wrote the play *Uncle Vanya*?

    A. Boris Pasternak
    B. Fyodor Dostoyevky
    C. Leo Tolstoy
    D. Anton Chekhov

29. In what year did ballet dancer Mikhail Baryshnikov defect to the United States?

    A. 1965
    B. 1974
    C. 1979
    D. 1984

30. Which ballet depicts the story of a young girl dreaming on Christmas Eve?

    A. *Swan Lake*
    B. *Giselle*
    C. *The Nutcracker*
    D. *La Sylphid*

31. What did Tom Brokaw title his 1999 best-selling history anthology?

    A. *The Century*
    B. *In Our Own Words*
    C. *Our Century*
    D. *The Greatest Generation*

32. The comic strip *Batman* is set in what city?

    A. Vatican City
    B. Gotham City
    C. Metropolis
    D. Philadelphia

33. In *A Christmas Carol*, how many ghosts visit Scrooge on Christmas Eve?

    A. 1
    B. 2
    C. 3
    D. 4

34. In Greek mythology, what was the monster with a human body and a bull's head who devoured the youth of Athens?

    A. Grendel
    B. Minotaur
    C. The Griffin
    D. Medusa

35. Which of these was *not* one of the Three Musketeers?

   A. Aramis
   B. Athos
   C. Porthos
   D. Bartholomew

36. What famous playwright documented the Salem witch trials in the award-winning play *The Crucible*?

   A. Neil Simon
   B. George Bernard Shaw
   C. Edward Albee
   D. Arthur Miller

37. Who published "The Rights of Man"?

   A. Thomas Paine
   B. W. E. B. Du Bois
   C. Frederick Douglas
   D. John Stuart Mill

38. What renowned feminist published the "Vindication of the Rights of Women" in 1792?

   A. Susan B. Anthony
   B. Gloria Steinem
   C. Mary Wollstonecraft
   D. Judith Butler

39. What philosopher and economist wrote the *Communist Manifesto* in 1848?

   A. David Hume
   B. John Stuart Mill
   C. Karl Marx
   D. Ludwig Von Mises

40. The South of France is home to what world-famous film festival?

    A. Arduois de Festival
    B. Sedona International
    C. Sundance
    D. Cannes Film Festival

41. Which film received 10 Oscars in 1960?

    A. *Lawrence of Arabia*
    B. *Ben-Hur*
    C. *Lion in Winter*
    D. *Inherit the Wind*

42. To what museum did Walter H. Annenberg donate his $1 billion art collection in 1991?

    A. Metropolitan Museum of Art
    B. Art Institute of Chicago
    C. National Gallery of Art
    D. Guggenheim Museum

43. Who were the two protagonists in Jane Austen's *Pride and Prejudice*?

    A. Darcy and Elizabeth
    B. Heathcliff and Catherine
    C. Rhett and Scarlett
    D. Rochester and Jane

44. Before showing up as spies in *The Adventures of Rocky and Bullwinkle*, who were Boris and Natasha?

    A. A Russian Czar and his wife
    B. Characters in *War and Peace*
    C. Stalin's cats
    D. A Russian folk dancing team

45. Who wrote *In Cold Blood*?

   A. Phillip Roth
   B. Tom Wolfe
   C. Bernard Malamud
   D. Truman Capote

46. Who performed Bill Clinton's campaign song at his inaugural ball?

   A. The Mamas and the Papas
   B. The Bee Gees
   C. The Eagles
   D. Fleetwood Mac

47. What episode in America's history did E. L. Doctrow examine in *The Book of Daniel*?

   A. The Great Depression
   B. The Rosenberg Trial
   C. Watergate
   D. Japanese Internment Camps

48. Who played the title role in *Mildred Pierce*?

   A. Bette Davis
   B. Marlene Dietrich
   C. Jane Wyman
   D. Joan Crawford

49. Which of the following authors is female?

   A. James Joyce
   B. T. S. Eliot
   C. C. S. Lewis
   D. George Eliot

50. Who wrote *I Know Why the Caged Bird Sings*?

A. Alice Walker
B. Maya Angelou
C. Toni Morrison
D. Terry McMillan

51. Which President was the subject of a biography titled *Dutch*?

A. Bill Clinton
B. George Bush
C. Ronald Reagan
D. Jimmy Carter

52. What was H. L. Mencken's profession?

A. Financier
B. Journalist
C. Politician
D. Attorney

53. According to the lyrics of Billy Joel's song, who "didn't start the fire"?

A. "We"
B. "You"
C. "I"
D. "Mrs. O'Leary's cow"

54. By what means would one go about conducting an epistolary relationship?

A. Making phone calls
B. Scheduling lunch dates
C. Writing letters
D. Meeting in church

55. What Russian author wrote *Crime and Punishment*?

    A. Gogol
    B. Tolstoy
    C. Pasternak
    D. Dostoyevsky

56. What is the cheapest available property on the classic board game *Monopoly*?

    A. Baltic
    B. Mediterranean
    C. Illinois
    D. Marvin Gardens

57. Who coined the phrase "turn on, tune in, and drop out"?

    A. Ken Kesey
    B. Jerry Garcia
    C. Tom Wolfe
    D. Timothy Leary

58. Which of the following teen movies was based upon a play by William Shakespeare?

    A. *Clueless*
    B. *Ten Things I Hate About You*
    C. *Can't Hardly Wait*
    D. *Never Been Kissed*

59. What European composer wrote "Bolero"?

    A. Arturo Toscanini
    B. Georges Bizet
    C. Maurice Ravel
    D. Igor Stravinsky

60. Which of the following classics of American literature was *not* the best-selling book of its year?

    A. *Grapes of Wrath*
    B. *Portnoy's Complaint*
    C. *All Quiet on the Western Front*
    D. *The Great Gatsby*

61. Most of Jane Austen's heroines come from which social class?

    A. Aristocracy
    B. Landed gentry
    C. Merchant/bourgeois
    D. Peasant

62. What kind of literary category does Marcel Proust's *Remembrance of Things Past* fall under?

    A. Memoir
    B. Poetry
    C. Novel
    D. Anthology

63. Which of the following philosophers was an early proponent of existentialism?

    A. Kierkegaard
    B. Karl Marx
    C. Spinoza
    D. Jean-Jacques Rousseau

64. What book was written by the author of *Around the World in Eighty Days*?

    A. *One Hundred Years of Solitude*
    B. *20,000 Leagues Under the Sea*
    C. *The Three Musketeers*
    D. *Catch-22*

65. Which of the following is not a disaster-at-sea movie?

   A. *The Poseidon Adventure*
   B. *Titanic*
   C. *Cabin Boy*
   D. *A Night to Remember*

66. What sculptor is famous for his mobiles?

   A. Gustave Rodin
   B. Henry Moore
   C. Alberto Giacometti
   D. Alexander Calder

67. Which writer's life did *not* end in suicide?

   A. Ernest Hemingway
   B. Virginia Woolf
   C. James Joyce
   D. Sylvia Plath

68. Which comic actor never made a silent film?

   A. Buster Keaton
   B. Jackie Gleason
   C. Charlie Chaplin
   D. Fatty Arbuckle

69. The Chicago skyline is commonly associated with what architect?

   A. Frank Lloyd Wright
   B. Alvar Aalto
   C. Le Corbusier
   D. Mies van der Rohe

70. The character of Shylock makes an appearance in what Shakespearean play?

   A. *Much Ado About Nothing*
   B. *The Tempest*
   C. *Taming of the Shrew*
   D. *Merchant of Venice*

71. Who said "A horse, a horse! My kingdom for a horse"?

   A. Othello
   B. Richard III
   C. Macbeth
   D. Henry VIII

72. Who sculpted the statue "The Fountain?"

   A. Marcel DuChamp
   B. Auguste Rodin
   C. Pablo Picasso
   D. Tommaso Solari

73. The "blue period" applies to what artist?

   A. Pablo Picasso
   B. Mary Cassatt
   C. Edward Degas
   D. Auguste Renoir

74. *The Legend of Sleepy Hollow* was written by what author?

   A. Washington Irving
   B. Nathaniel Hawthorne
   C. Mary Shelley
   D. Steven Crane

75. What monster did author Bram Stoker create?

    A. The Vampire Lestat
    B. Frankenstein
    C. Count Dracula
    D. The Headless Horseman

76. What famous poet had a club foot?

    A. Lord Byron
    B. William Shakespeare
    C. Henry Longfellow
    D. William Wordsworth

77. Samuel Clemens was the real name of which famous American author?

    A. Edgar Allen Poe
    B. Mark Twain
    C. Ernest Hemingway
    D. William Faulkner

78. How many fairy tales did brothers Jakob and Wilhelm Grimm write?

    A. 134
    B. 178
    C. 211
    D. 264

79. What color was the tablecloth in Leonardo da Vinci's painting *The Last Supper*?

    A. Red
    B. Blue
    C. White
    D. Yellow

80. What was Snow White's coffin made of?

    A. Glass
    B. Grass
    C. Flowers
    D. Cement

81. What natural substance are violin strings made of?

    A. Horsehair
    B. Human hair
    C. Angora
    D. Wool

82. How long did it take Handel to write the score for *The Messiah*?

    A. 1 week
    B. 3 weeks
    C. 2 months
    D. 1 year

83. What famous painting did Francis I of France buy to hang in his bathroom?

    A. "Starry Night"
    B. "The Last Supper"
    C. "Mona Lisa"
    D. "The Birth of Venus"

84. *Cocksucker Blues* was a film about what rock group?

    A. The Ramones
    B. The Clash
    C. The Scorpions
    D. The Rolling Stones

85. The film *Cleopatra* was banned in what country in 1963?

   A. Turkey
   B. France
   C. Egypt
   D. Iran

86. What was the group B-52s named after?

   A. A soft drink
   B. A hair style
   C. An engine
   D. A bicycle

87. What was the subject of the first printed book in England?

   A. Birds
   B. Antique books
   C. Chess
   D. Farming

88. What celebrity canine is buried in Paris' Pere-Lachaise cemetery?

   A. Benji
   B. Rin-Tin-Tin
   C. Lassie
   D. Old Yeller

89. What famous bluesman owns a guitar named "Lucille"?

   A. Buddy Guy
   B. Otis Redding
   C. B. B. King
   D. Stevie Ray Vaughan

90. How many Oscars was Walt Disney awarded between the years 1931 and 1969?

   A. 25
   B. 35
   C. 45
   D. 55

91. In *Romeo and Juliet*, the "wherefore" in "Wherefore art thou, Romeo" means what?

   A. Where
   B. Why
   C. When
   D. What

92. In the original story, what were Cinderella's slippers made of?

   A. Leather
   B. Diamonds
   C. Fur
   D. Pearl

93. Where is the largest organ in the world located?

   A. Las Vegas
   B. Vatican City
   C. Notre Dame Church
   D. Atlantic City

94. Which of the following did Giacomo Puccini *not* compose?

   A. *La Boheme*
   B. *Madama Butterfly*
   C. *Tosca*
   D. *La Traviata*

95. In what decade were the first Academy Awards held?

   A. 1910s
   B. 1920s
   C. 1930s
   D. 1940s

96. The *William Tell* Overture was the theme music for which television show?

   A. *The Love Boat*
   B. *The Lone Ranger*
   C. *The Avengers*
   D. *The Magnificent Seven*

97. What leading man was born Issur Danielovitch Demsky on December, 9, 1916?

   A. James Cagney
   B. Humphrey Bogart
   C. Kirk Douglas
   D. Marlon Brando

98. Whose false eyelashes were sold for $125 in a 1979 auction?

   A. Marylin Monroe
   B. Judy Garland
   C. Marlene Deitrich
   D. Vivian Leigh

99. What poet responsible for "The Rime of the Ancient Mariner," was addicted to opium in the latter part of his life?

A. Samuel Taylor Coleridge
B. William Blake
C. Lord Byron
D. Walt Whitman

100. For which play did George Bernard Shaw refuse to accept an Oscar?

A. *Saint Joan*
B. *Mrs. Warren's Profession*
C. *Pygmalion*
D. *Candida*

101. Steve Martin earned his first starring role in what movie?

A. *All of Me*
B. *The Jerk*
C. *Three Amigos*
D. *Roxanne*

102. The musical *West Side Story* was based on which Shakespearean play?

A. *Love's Labor Lost*
B. *Midsummer Night's Dream*
C. *Romeo and Juliet*
D. *Merchant of Venice*

103. What actress was dubbed "the statue of libido"?

A. Jean Harlow
B. Mae West
C. Brigitte Bardot
D. Veronica Lake

104. Frank Baum is the author of what popular children's book?

   A. *Alice in Wonderland*
   B. *The Wizard of Oz*
   C. *Cinderella*
   D. *Peter Pan*

105. Which of the following is not one of Stephen King's books?

   A. *The Shining*
   B. *Thinner*
   C. *A Nightmare on Elm Street*
   D. *Carrie*

106. What is the protagonist in Franz Kafka's *The Metamorphosis* transformed into?

   A. Insect
   B. Dog
   C. Little boy
   D. Tree

107. Eric Arthur Blair was the pen name for what author?

   A. Douglas Coupland
   B. Don DeLillo
   C. George Orwell
   D. Aldous Huxley

108. What happened to Ophelia in Shakespeare's play *Hamlet*?

   A. Became queen
   B. Committed suicide
   C. Lived happily ever after
   D. Opened an orphanage

109. How many tales did Chaucer include in the *Canterbury Tales?*

    A. 24
    B. 29
    C. 35
    D. 38

110. Who wrote *The Jungle Book?*

    A. Rudyard Kipling
    B. Joseph Conrad
    C. Sylvia Plath
    D. Lewis Carroll

111. Squire Trelawney is a character in what book?

    A. *The Three Musketeers*
    B. *Gulliver's Travels*
    C. *Treasure Island*
    D. *Dr. Jekyll and Mr. Hyde*

112. Eeyore and Kanga are characters in what children's book?

    A. *Peter Pan*
    B. *Winnie the Pooh*
    C. *Curious George*
    D. *The Jungle Book*

113. William Claude Dunkenfield was the real name of which famous performer?

    A. Fred Astaire
    B. Andy Rooney
    C. W. C. Fields
    D. Charlie Chaplin

114. What Greek male figure was known for his beauty and hazardous affair with Aphrodite?

    A. Adonis
    B. Achilles
    C. Orpheus
    D. Perseus

115. "All the world's a stage" is a quote from what Shakespearean play?

    A. *As You Like It*
    B. *Love's Labours Lost*
    C. *Merchant of Venice*
    D. *Macbeth*

116. The Artful Dodger is a character from what Charles Dickens novel?

    A. *Hard Times*
    B. *A Tale of Two Cities*
    C. *Oliver Twist*
    D. *Great Expectations*

117. Which American wrote the famous poem *Song of Myself*?

    A. Robert Frost
    B. Adrienne Rich
    C. Henry David Thoreau
    D. Walt Whitman

118. The epic poem *Paradise Lost* was written by what English poet?

    A. John Milton
    B. Sir Walter Scott
    C. Lord Alfred Tennyson
    D. Henry Wadsworth Longfellow

119. What artist created Betty Boop in 1915?

    A. Jim Davis
    B. Max Fleischer
    C. Garry B. Trudeau
    D. Bill Watterson

120. What was the name of Jay Gatsby's love interest in F. Scott Fitzgerald's novel *The Great Gatsby?*

    A. Penelope
    B. Daisy
    C. Sarah
    D. Betty

CHAPTER SEVEN

SPORTS

1. In what year did Native American Jim Thorpe win the Olympic gold medal for both the decathlon and pentathlon?

   A. 1904
   B. 1912
   C. 1920
   D. 1928

2. What team did the New York Rangers lose to in the 1950 Stanley Cup finals?

   A. Detroit Red Wings
   B. Chicago Black Hawks
   C. Montreal Canadians
   D. Toronto Maple Leafs

3. For how long does a cowboy in a rodeo bull riding event need to hang on in order to qualify?

   A. 8 seconds
   B. 12 seconds
   C. 16 seconds
   D. 20 seconds

4. According to recent studies, champions from which sport have the highest average age?

A. Golf
B. Billiards
C. Bowling
D. Tennis

5. Following his 1997 attack on Evander Holyfield, the Hollywood Wax Museum moved boxer Mike Tyson's replica next to which waxwork?

A. Dr. Hannibal Lecter
B. Dr. Kevorkian
C. O. J. Simpson
D. Jack the Ripper

6. What part of his body does a professional football player have the highest chance of injuring?

A. Neck
B. Spine
C. Knee
D. Elbow

7. What baseball player holds the record for the longest complete game victory?

A. Reggie Jackson
B. Babe Ruth
C. Yogi Berra
D. Burleigh Grimes

8. What sport was first recognized as an official sport in the 1992 Olympic Summer Games?

   A. Women's soccer
   B. Synchronized swimming
   C. Badminton
   D. Archery

9. Which of the following is not a type of tennis court playing surface?

   A. Clay court
   B. Soft court
   C. Hard court
   D. Grass

10. The Los Angeles Dodgers originally hailed from what New York borough?

   A. Queens
   B. Staten Island
   C. Bronx
   D. Brooklyn

11. In what country was the first baseball game first televised?

   A. United States
   B. Canada
   C. Japan
   D. Brazil

12. Who was the only tennis pro to be disqualified from both the Grand Slam and Australian Open tournaments for misconduct?

    A. Andre Agassi
    B. John McEnroe
    C. Boris Becker
    D. Patrick Rafter

13. How many rings interlock to form the Olympic symbol?

    A. 3
    B. 4
    C. 5
    D. 6

14. What does the baseball term "can of corn" refer to?

    A. A foul ball
    B. A strike
    C. A poor player
    D. A fly ball

15. What sport was *never* an official Olympic event?

    A. Tug of war
    B. Table Tennis
    C. Scrabble
    D. Handball

16. What boxer was featured on the cover of the Beatles album *Sgt. Pepper's Lonely Hearts Club Band*?

    A. Muhammad Ali
    B. Sonny Liston
    C. Sugar Ray Leonard
    D. Joe Louis

17. Which jockey rode to two Triple Crown wins on Whirlaway in 1941 and on Citation in 1948?

    A. Bill Hartack
    B. Willie Shoemaker
    C. Pat Day
    D. Eddie Arcaro

18. In what year did the New York Yankees win their fifth consecutive World Series championship title?

    A. 1951
    B. 1952
    C. 1953
    D. 1954

19. How long are professional Golf Tour players allotted per shot?

    A. 25 seconds
    B. 45 seconds
    C. 1 minute
    D. 2 minutes

20. What is the oldest stadium still in use in the NFL?

    A. Soldier Field
    B. Giants Stadium
    C. Rooney Field
    D. Oakland Coliseum

21. What is the only sport that looks backward in a mirror?

    A. Hockey
    B. Basketball
    C. Baseball
    D. Football

22. Who is the only NBA player to win four consecutive NBA championships?

   A. Steve Karr
   B. Michael Jordan
   C. Magic Johnson
   D. Bill Russell

23. Which of the following was *not* one of Michael Jordan's basketball numbers?

   A. 9
   B. 12
   C. 23
   D. 54

24. What basketball star won the NBA's MVP award in 1984, 1985, and 1986?

   A. Charles Barkley
   B. Larry Bird
   C. Kareem Abdul-Jabar
   D. Magic Johnson

25. What is the largest stadium in the NFL?

   A. Mile High Stadium
   B. Georgia Dome
   C. Oakland Coliseum
   D. Pontiac Silverdome

26. Who is the only major league umpire to be inducted in both the baseball and football hall of fame?

   A. Jocko Conlan
   B. Billy Evans
   C. Cal Hubbard
   D. Bill Clemm

27. How is a forfeited baseball game recorded?

    A. 1-0
    B. 2-0
    C. 7-0
    D. 9-0

28. Who was the only baseball player to hit four home runs in one game and three triples in another?

    A. Willie Mays
    B. Hank Aaron
    C. Rod Carew
    D. Jim Palmer

29. Which team holds the record for winning the most games without a loss?

    A. Chicago Blackhawks
    B. The Philadelphia Flyers
    C. New York Yankees
    D. Los Angeles Lakers

30. What is the highest "par" approved by the United States Golf Association?

    A. 4
    B. 5
    C. 6
    D. 7

31. Who is responsible for throwing the most consecutive completed passes in a Super Bowl game?

    A. Joe Namath
    B. Joe Montana
    C. Walter Payton
    D. Johnny Unitas

32. Sammy Sosa originally hails from which country?

    A. Cuba
    B. Venezuela
    C. Honduras
    D. Dominican Republic

33. How many laps are driven in the Indy 500?

    A. 100
    B. 200
    C. 300
    D. 400

34. How wide is a regulation-size soccer goal?

    A. 20 feet
    B. 22 feet
    C. 24 feet
    D. 26 feet

35. What is Canada's official national sport?

    A. Polo
    B. Hockey
    C. Soccer
    D. Lacrosse

36. The Dallas Cowboys played in how many Super Bowls?

    A. 5
    B. 6
    C. 7
    D. 8

37. Where were the first Winter Olympics held?

   A. Chamonix, France
   B. Alberta, Canada
   C. Stockholm, Sweden
   D. Oslo, Norway

38. The Football Hall of Fame is located in what state?

   A. Ohio
   B. Michigan
   C. Illinois
   D. New York

39. What golfer has won a total of four U.S. Open tournaments?

   A. Arnold Palmer
   B. Jack Nicklaus
   C. Tiger Woods
   D. Byron Nelson

40. Who is the youngest player ever inducted into the Football Hall of Fame?

   A. Dick Butkus
   B. Joe Greene
   C. Gale Sayers
   D. Joe Namath

41. Who was the first sports star to have his number retired?

   A. Lou Gehrig
   B. Babe Ruth
   C. Willie Mays
   D. Yogi Berra

42. What is Alaska's official state sport?

    A. Sledding
    B. Ice skating
    C. Dog-mushing
    D. Hockey

43. In what year did Bert Bell begin what is now known as the NFL draft?

    A. 1922
    B. 1936
    C. 1943
    D. 1948

44. Which Chicago sports team was nicknamed "the Monsters of the Midway" in 1939?

    A. The Bulls
    B. The Bears
    C. The Cubs
    D. The White Sox

45. Which football hero was nicknamed "The Sundance Kid"?

    A. Troy Aikman
    B. Jim Kiick
    C. Brett Favre
    D. Joe Montana

46. Who bought the New York Yankees in 1973?

    A. George Steinbrenner
    B. Billy Martin
    C. Ted Turner
    D. Bill Veeck

47. Which famous baseball player said, "It ain't over, till it's over"?

   A. Babe Ruth
   B. Yogi Berra
   C. Reggi Jackson
   D. Mickey Mantle

48. Who was the first woman to win Olympic Gold for tennis?

   A. Charlotte Cooper
   B. Anke Huber
   C. Sarah Pitkowski
   D. Nicole Pratt

49. In what country was the first Grand Prix held?

   A. Germany
   B. Spain
   C. France
   D. United States

50. Which country hosted and won the first football World Cup?

   A. Argentina
   B. Uruguay
   C. Ecuador
   D. Guyana

51. What car was driven to first place by Lee Petty in the first Indy 500?

   A. Chevrolet
   B. Dodge
   C. Mercedes
   D. Oldsmobile

52. Who made the first solo climb to the top of Mount Everest?

   A. Peter Habeler
   B. Reinhold Messner
   C. Shambu Tamang
   D. Edmund Hillary

53. What boxer stopped Hector Mercedes in his professional debut in 1985?

   A. Mike Tyson
   B. Jack Dempsey
   C. Rocky Marciano
   D. Jake LaMotta

54. What was the dollar figure of the contract signed by Babe Ruth in 1930?

   A. $30K
   B. $50K
   C. $80K
   D. $120K

55. In what year did the Orlando Magic set an NBA record by hitting at least one three-pointer for 210 consecutive games?

   A. 1994
   B. 1995
   C. 1996
   D. 1997

56. Who was the first NBA player to score 2,000 points in one season?

    A. George Yardley
    B. Kareem Abdul-Jabbar
    C. Wilt Chamberlain
    D. Bill Bradley

57. After knocking down his opponent Jim Corbett, what boxer was quoted as saying, "The bigger they are, the harder they fall"?

    A. Joe Frazier
    B. Bob Fitzsimmons
    C. Sugar Ray Leonard
    D. Joe Louis

58. Who is the youngest tennis player to win a women's tennis tournament at the age of 13?

    A. Anna Kournikova
    B. Steffi Graf
    C. Jennifer Capriati
    D. Kristina Brandi

59. What California city hosts the tournament of roses parade?

    A. Oakland
    B. Modesto
    C. Los Angeles
    D. Pasadena

60. What team won the first Rose Bowl in 1902?

    A. Michigan
    B. Stanford
    C. Tulane
    D. Illinois

61. The New York Jets recruited Joe Namath from which university for a reported $400,000?

   A. University of Arkansas
   B. Michigan State
   C. University of Alabama
   D. University of Southern California

62. Where were the 1996 Summer Olympics held?

   A. Barcelona
   B. Atlanta
   C. Athens
   D. Sydney

63. Bill Russell played defensive center for what basketball team?

   A. Boston Celtics
   B. Chicago Bulls
   C. New York Knicks
   D. L.A. Lakers

64. Which boxer changed his name from Cassius Clay?

   A. Muhammed Ali
   B. George Foreman
   C. Sugar Ray Leonard
   D. Joe Lewis

65. Which sporting good was introduced to the U.S. in 1957?

   A. Boomerang
   B. Trampoline
   C. Frisbee
   D. Running shoes

66. What is the hockey term for scoring three goals in one game?

   A. Slide Stick
   B. Hat Trick
   C. Three Pointer
   D. Ice Chip

67. What sport is Dr. James Naismith credited with inventing?

   A. Baseball
   B. Basketball
   C. Hockey
   D. Polo

68. Which of these four tennis events are *not* part of the Grand Slam?

   A. The French Open
   B. Wimbeldon
   C. U.S. Open
   D. Davis Cup

69. What is the height of a tabletennis net?

   A. 3 inches
   B. 4 inches
   C. 5 inches
   D. 6 inches

70. The film *Days of Thunder* depicted which sport?

   A. Skiiing
   B. Football
   C. Car racing
   D. Rollerblading

71. What player became the youngest chess grand master at the age of fourteen?

   A. Etienne Bacrat
   B. Boris Spassky
   C. Robert Fischer
   D. Antoly Karpov

72. The first screwball was thrown in what decade?

   A. 1920
   B. 1930
   C. 1940
   D. 1950

73. The Mavericks are based in what city?

   A. Washington
   B. Sacramento
   C. Cleveland
   D. Dallas

74. What college sports team has won the most Orange Bowls?

   A. Penn State
   B. Miami
   C. Oklahoma
   D. Nebraska

75. In what year did Jeff Gordon win his first Daytona 500?

   A. 1994
   B. 1995
   C. 1996
   D. 1997

76. Which of these basketball players has *not* earned five season MVP awards?

   A. Michael Jordan
   B. Bill Russell
   C. Larry Bird
   D. Kareem Abdul-Jabbar

77. What team has gone 92 years since winning a World Series title?

   A. Chicago Cubs
   B. Baltimore Orioles
   C. Seattle Mariners
   D. Houston Astros

78. Who holds the career record for hitting two or more home runs in the most games?

   A. Babe Ruth
   B. Bill Hamilton
   C. Lou Gehrig
   D. Hank Aaron

79. Babe Ruth played his last Major League game for what team?

   A. New York Yankees
   B. Atlanta Braves
   C. New York Mets
   D. Texas Rangers

80. What team hosted the first night game?

   A. San Diego Padres
   B. Baltimore Orioles
   C. Philadelphia Phillies
   D. Cincinnati Reds

81. What team was the first to feature names on the back of their uniforms?

    A. New York Yankees
    B. St. Louis Cardinals
    C. Chicago White Sox
    D. Boston Red Sox

82. Which team was first to win three Super Bowls?

    A. Pittsburgh Steelers
    B. Washington Redskins
    C. Green Bay Packers
    D. Dallas Cowboys

83. Who broke Earl Cooper's record for receptions by a rookie?

    A. Terry Glen
    B. Jim Rice
    C. Steve Ingram
    D. Tiki Barber

84. In what year did Jim Brown retire?

    A. 1963
    B. 1966
    C. 1969
    D. 1972

85. In what city did the Dallas Cowboys lose three Super Bowls?

    A. Pasadena
    B. New Orleans
    C. Miami
    D. Los Angeles

86. Who did the Oakland Raiders lose to in Super Bowl II?

    A. Green Bay Packers
    B. Oilers
    C. Miami Dolphins
    D. Minnesota Vikings

87. The Bucs traded Steve Young to what team?

    A. San Francisco 49ers
    B. Indianapolis Colts
    C. St. Louis Rams
    D. Oakland Raiders

88. Who was the youngest player to be inducted into the Pro Football Hall of Fame?

    A. Gale Sayers
    B. Jim Brown
    C. Dick Butkus
    D. Jimmy Johnson

89. What team holds the record for losing the most NFL championship games?

    A. New York Giants
    B. Chicago Bears
    C. Cleveland Browns
    D. San Francisco 49ers

90. Figure skating became an Olympic event in what year?

    A. 1904
    B. 1908
    C. 1912
    D. 1916

91. Besides Brazil, what country has won soccer's World Cup three times?

    A. Italy
    B. France
    C. Argentina
    D. Germany

92. What player was the first to receive two busts in the Pro Football Hall of Fame?

    A. Mike Ditka
    B. Frank Gifford
    C. Stan Jones
    D. Joe Namath

93. What nation saw its golfers go on to win the first 16 U.S. Opens?

    A. United States
    B. Britain
    C. Canada
    D. Ireland

94. Bowling was first played in what country?

    A. France
    B. United States
    C. Japan
    D. Germany

95. Name the first team to lose the first two games in the finals and win four consecutive games for the title?

    A. Boston Celtics
    B. Portland Trail Blazers
    C. New York Knicks
    D. Chicago Bulls

96. In archery, how many points is a bull's-eye worth?

   A. 7
   B. 9
   C. 11
   D. 13

97. In what country did bobsledding make its first appearance?

   A. France
   B. Belgium
   C. Switzerland
   D. United States

98. In what year were the Olympics first televised?

   A. 1952
   B. 1956
   C. 1960
   D. 1964

99. Which of the following Grand Slam championships did Jimmy Connors *not* win?

   A. French Open
   B. Australian Open
   C. Wimbledon
   D. U.S. Open

100. What sports competition awards its winners the Vince Lombardi Trophy?

   A. Tour de France
   B. Orange Bowl
   C. Super Bowl
   D. World Cup

101. Who is the youngest male tennis player to win the U.S. Open?

    A. Boris Becker
    B. Pete Sampras
    C. Bill Tilden
    D. Michael Chang

102. What country hosted the 1998 Winter Olympics?

    A. Germany
    B. United States
    C. Japan
    D. Finland

103. Who is the only defensive player from the losing team to win the MVP in a Super Bowl?

    A. Alan Page
    B. Deion Sanders
    C. Chuck Howley
    D. Bubba Smith

104. What basketball player was born in New York but grew up in North Carolina?

    A. Charles Barkley
    B. Julius Irving
    C. Michael Jordan
    D. Karl Malone

105. Which of the following films did Micky Mantle *not* appear in?

    A. *Safe at Home*
    B. *Bull Durham*
    C. *That Touch of Mink*
    D. *It's My Turn*

106. Who broke Babe Ruth's home run record with 715?

    A. Norm Cash
    B. Lou Gehrig
    C. Hank Aaron
    D. Sammy Sosa

107. In what year did Roger Maris hit 61 home runs?

    A. 1959
    B. 1961
    C. 1963
    D. 1965

108. "Wild Bull of the Pampas" was the nickname for what heavyweight boxer?

    A. Sonny Liston
    B. Mike Tyson
    C. Louis Firpo
    D. Tommy Burns

109. What football player received credit for the "immaculate reception"?

    A. Franco Harris
    B. Steve Largent
    C. Joe Namath
    D. Don Hutson

110. Who has the most titles in the WWF?

    A. Bret Hart
    B. Shawn Michaels
    C. Steve Austin
    D. Hulk Hogan

111. What hockey player holds the single season scoring record?

    A. Eric Lindros
    B. Phil Espisito
    C. Mark Messier
    D. Wayne Gretzky

112. In what round did Joe Lewis beat out Jimmy Ellis to become the world champ in 1970?

    A. 4th
    B. 5th
    C. 6th
    D. 7th

113. What golfer won the U.S. Open in 1996?

    A. Tom Lehman
    B. Steve Jones
    C. Mark Brooks
    D. Nick Faldo

114. Who holds the record for being the all-time career leader in knockouts?

    A. Archie Moore
    B. Jack Johnson
    C. Tommy Burns
    D. Gene Tunney

115. What male tennis player has won the most Grand Slam titles?

    A. Rod Laver
    B. Bill Tilden
    C. Roy Emerson
    D. Bjorn Borg

116. Who was the first winner of the Indy 500?

    A. Tom Sneva
    B. Lee Petty
    C. Richard Petty
    D. Jackie Stewart

117. Who won the first women's Olympic Marathon?

    A. Rosa Mota
    B. Mary Decker
    C. Joan Benoit
    D. Greta Waitz

118. What team holds the record for consecutive games lost in the Super Bowl?

    A. Kansas City Chiefs
    B. Buffalo Bills
    C. Minnesota Vikings
    D. San Francisco 49ers

119. What country has lost the most World Cup Titles games?

    A. Spain
    B. Italy
    C. United States
    D. Germany

120. The first NCAA men's college basketball championship was won by what team?

    A. Syracuse University
    B. Penn State
    C. University of Michigan
    D. University of Oregon

CHAPTER EIGHT

SCIENCE AND TECHNOLOGY

1. On average, how many times do the eye muscles move a day?

   A. 10,000
   B. 50,000
   C. 100,000
   D. 200,000

2. What are the three primary colors?

   A. Red, yellow, and blue
   B. Red, orange, and green
   C. Red, blue, and purple
   D. Red, green, and blue

3. What famous diet swept the nation in 1978?

   A. The Pritikin Diet
   B. The Atkins Diet Revolution
   C. The Scarsdale Diet
   D. The Juice Fast

4. What animal benefited from the first artificial heart implant in 1957?

   A. Baboon
   B. Sheep
   C. Dog
   D. Cow

5. In what year was the World Wide Web introduced?

   A. 1981
   B. 1985
   C. 1989
   D. 1991

6. What is the offspring called of a male horse and female donkey?

   A. Mule
   B. Donkey
   C. Hinny
   D. Colt

7. The consumption of what food can make you a target for mosquitoes?

   A. Strawberries
   B. Apples
   C. Lemons
   D. Bananas

8. A castrated rooster is otherwise known as a ...

   A. Castrata
   B. Capon
   C. Raster
   D. Eunuch

9. Which of these insects never sleeps?

   A. Flies
   B. Moths
   C. Ants
   D. Mosquitoes

10. What former presidential candidate lent his support to Viagra endorsements?

    A. Ross Perot
    B. Al Gore
    C. Bob Dole
    D. Michael Dukakis

11. What is the only animal immune from every disease, including cancer?

    A. Shark
    B. Dolphin
    C. Crocodile
    D. Alligator

12. What covers ⅛ of the earth's surface?

    A. Sand
    B. Water
    C. Ice
    D. Vegetation

13. A person who has taphephobia is scared of what?

    A. Large, open spaces
    B. Being buried alive
    C. Heights
    D. Spiders

14. Which of these inventors created the escalator in 1900?

A. Johaan Valer
B. Charles Seeberger
C. Horace Short
D. Willis Carrier

15. Which of the following is the smallest measure of time?

A. Yoctosecond
B. Minisecond
C. Demisecond
D. Nanosecond

16. In what decade did the Concorde jet make its first trial flight?

A. 1950
B. 1960
C. 1970
D. 1980

17. A speleologist is an expert in what field of study?

A. Words spellings
B. Birds
C. Caves
D. Insects

18. What is the name for the white part of a fingernail?

A. Philtrim
B. Verean
C. Lunula
D. Aglets

19. What pain medication was advertised as containing heroine in 1982?

    A. Bayer
    B. Excedrin
    C. Tylenol
    D. Aspirin

20. Which of these inventions was *not* created by a woman?

    A. Fire escapes
    B. Bulletproof vests
    C. Post-It Notes
    D. Windshield wipers

21. What is IBM's long-standing motto?

    A. Imagine
    B. Explore
    C. Think
    D. Create

22. In what year did the first personal computer, Apple II, come on the market?

    A. 1974
    B. 1977
    C. 1981
    D. 1984

23. Which of these is the only metal that is liquid in room temperature?

    A. Aluminum
    B. Copper
    C. Mercury
    D. Pewter

24. Stalagmites and stalactites are types of what?

   A. Mineral deposits
   B. Rocks
   C. Sea weeds
   D. Greek columns

25. What herb has been widely used in Germany to combat depression and is only now gaining popularity in the U.S.?

   A. Chamomile
   B. St. John's Wort
   C. Ginsing
   D. Melatonin

26. What animal's heart weighs 25 pounds and is two feet long?

   A. Tiger
   B. Elephant
   C. Hippopotamus
   D. Giraffe

27. What is commonly known as a "winkle"?

   A. A short nap
   B. A sea snail
   C. A little mouse
   D. A sneeze

28. A cat uses it's whiskers for what purpose?

   A. Measuring small spaces
   B. Cleaning
   C. Establishing authority
   D. Tracking its prey

29. Which of these mammals is the heaviest, sometimes weighing up to 8,000 pounds?

    A. Elephant
    B. Giraffe
    C. Lion
    D. Hippopotamus

30. What animal can climb trees faster than it can run on the ground?

    A. Mice
    B. Koala Bears
    C. Squirrels
    D. Monkeys

31. What sea creature is comprised of 95 percent water and has no brain, heart, or bones?

    A. Starfish
    B. Jellyfish
    C. Squid
    D. Octopus

32. What is the only bird that can fly backward?

    A. Hummingbird
    B. Sparrow
    C. Eagle
    D. Pigeon

33. How many different muscles are there in a bird's wing?

    A. 10
    B. 20
    C. 30
    D. 40

34. What is a "kakapo" a type of?

    A. Hat
    B. Parrot
    C. Seaweed
    D. Boat

35. What bird has been seen flying at altitudes of 27,000 feet, higher than any other bird on record?

    A. Swan
    B. Eagle
    C. Geese
    D. Crane

36. A cow can't give milk until it has . . .

    A. Been sterilized
    B. Given birth
    C. Reached a certain age
    D. Copulated

37. On average, how many glasses of milk will a cow produce in a lifetime?

    A. 50,000
    B. 100,000
    C. 200,000
    D. 300,000

38. Which of these is *not* a term for a group of bees?

    A. Swarm
    B. Cluster
    C. Hive
    D. Grist

39. What animal uses its tail to jump through the air?

   A. Fox
   B. Antelope
   C. Kangaroo
   D. Skunk

40. A pair of rats can produce up to how many babies in one year?

   A. 50
   B. 500
   C. 1,500
   D. 15,000

41. What is the only mammal that is able to fly?

   A. Squirrel
   B. Rat
   C. Bat
   D. Opossum

42. What kind of building can a rat fall from without sustaining any injuries?

   A. 2-story
   B. 3-story
   C. 4-story
   D. 5-story

43. Snakes use their tongues for what purpose?

   A. Feeling
   B. Seeing
   C. Hearing
   D. Smelling

44. What do camels have three of to protect themselves from the sand?

    A. Humps
    B. Ear flaps
    C. Nostrils
    D. Eyelids

45. Approximately how many years does it take a lobster to weigh one pound?

    A. 2 years
    B. 5 years
    C. 7 years
    D. 10 years

46. Dogs sweat through their . . .

    A. Paws
    B. Skin
    C. Tongue
    D. Forehead

47. Why do bulls charge when they see a red cape?

    A. The color red irritates their cornea
    B. They respond to the movement of the cape
    C. They equate the color red with blood
    D. The color causes vibrations in their nose

48. What is the gaffer's main responsibility on a film set?

    A. Running errands
    B. Cinematography
    C. Electricity
    D. Set design

49. From where do 70 to 80 percent of all olives come from?

   A. California
   B. Mexico
   C. Italy
   D. France

50. What natural disaster is responsible for killing more people in the U.S. than any other, with 400 deaths and 1000 injuries per year?

   A. Tornado
   B. Flooding
   C. Hurricane
   D. Lightning

51. What is the highest type of cloud formation, occurring at an average altitude of 27,000 feet?

   A. Cirrus
   B. Cumulus
   C. Stratus
   D. Nimbus

52. On what side are the rings of a tree usually spaced farthest apart?

   A. Northern
   B. Southern
   C. Eastern
   D. Western

53. What is the only continent without reptiles or snakes?

    A. Antarctica
    B. Australia
    C. Africa
    D. Europe

54. Which of these four U.S. states is not home to an active volcano?

    A. Washington
    B. California
    C. Alaska
    D. Colorado

55. The size of your foot is approximately the size of which body part?

    A. Thigh
    B. Forearm
    C. Calf
    D. Upper arm

56. What is the most common blood type in the world?

    A. A
    B. B
    C. AB
    D. O

57. Which of the following is not an organ?

    A. Liver
    B. Heart
    C. Kidney
    D. Brain

58. Who invented the telephone?

   A. Thomas Edison
   B. Alexander Graham Bell
   C. Benjamin Franklin
   D. Orville Wright

59. Who invented the vaccine for polio in 1952?

   A. Marie Curie
   B. Ian Fleming
   C. Jonas Salk
   D. Louis Pasteur

60. What happens to time as it nears a black hole?

   A. It accelerates
   B. It stops
   C. It slows down
   D. It runs backward

61. What is the largest planet in the solar system?

   A. Mars
   B. Mercury
   C. Neptune
   D. Jupiter

62. What Internet provider features the greeting "You've Got Mail"?

   A. Earthlink
   B. AOL
   C. Compuserve
   D. Yahoo

63. In order to qualify as a skyscraper, how tall must a building be?

    A. 300 feet
    B. 500 feet
    C. 700 feet
    D. 900 feet

64. Before they became famous for creating the Apple computer, Steve Jobs and Steve Wozniak invented what popular computer game?

    A. Pac-Man
    B. Frogger
    C. Kaboom
    D. Breakout

65. What is the heaviest inert gas?

    A. Helium
    B. Xenon
    C. Radon
    D. Argon

66. What were the first living creatures sent into space?

    A. Mice
    B. Monkeys
    C. Cats
    D. Fish

67. Which of the following is *not* one of the three body types classified by William Sheldon in 1935?

    A. Endomorph
    B. Tendomorph
    C. Mesomorph
    D. Ectomorph

68. What was the name of the first cloned sheep?

    A. Holly
    B. Sally
    C. Dolly
    D. Kelly

69. Planets and stars are mostly made of what substance?

    A. Nitrogen
    B. Helium
    C. Hydrogen
    D. Oxygen

70. What mathematician is otherwise known as "the father of geometry"?

    A. Pythagoras
    B. Euclid
    C. Pascal
    D. Copernicus

71. What scientist espoused the principle of natural selection in *The Origin of Species*?

    A. Charles Darwin
    B. Galileo Galilei
    C. Gregor Mendel
    D. Luis Alvarez

72. Which of the following is *not* a space-related phenomenon?

    A. Black hole
    B. Wormhole
    C. Red hole
    D. White hole

73. Who discovered that the rings of Saturn are divided into two parts?

    A. Galileo Galilei
    B. Cassini
    C. Christian Huygens
    D. Nicholaus Copernicus

74. What is the clinical term for the inside of a human's mouth?

    A. Mandible
    B. Pulp
    C. Buccal cavity
    D. Maxillae

75. What kind of clouds generally produce hail?

    A. Cirrus
    B. Cumulonimbus
    C. Orographic
    D. Lenticular

76. What part of a computer does Mhz apply to?

    A. Processor
    B. Hard drive
    C. Mouse
    D. Track pad

77. A doctor uses what kind of instrument to test a patient's reflexes?

    A. Plessor
    B. Alameter
    C. Rimformer
    D. Otoscope

78. What does the computer acronym RAM stand for?

   A. Remote Access Memory
   B. Random Application Monitor
   C. Remote Application Monitor
   D. Random Access Memory

79. Which plane relies completely on its avionics systems?

   A. Boeing 777
   B. McDonnell Douglas DC10
   C. Concorde
   D. Airbus 330

80. What spacecraft uncovered a small moon orbiting the asteroid Ida?

   A. *Magellan*
   B. *Galileo*
   C. *Ulysses*
   D. *Viking*

81. What element makes up the majority of Uranus' atmosphere?

   A. Hydrogen
   B. Helium
   C. Methane
   D. Nitrogen

82. Russian scientist Mikhail Lomonosov discovered the atmosphere of what planet in 1761?

   A. Mars
   B. Pluto
   C. Jupiter
   D. Venus

83. What did Jean de Rosier and the Marquis d'Arlandes fly for the first time 500 feet above Paris in 1783?

    A. Kite
    B. Hot-air balloon
    C. Blimp
    D. Paper airplane

84. Who invented the printing press?

    A. Eli Whitney
    B. Johannes Gutenberg
    C. Robert J. Seiwald
    D. Thomas Jefferson

85. Who invented the self-contained underwater breathing apparatus (SCUBA)?

    A. Jacques-Yves Cousteau
    B. Thomas Adams
    C. Edwin Howard Armstrong
    D. Thomas Edison

86. Which scientist proposed the theory of relativity?

    A. Stephen Hawking
    B. Albert Einstein
    C. Charles Darwin
    D. Isaac Newton

87. Psychiatrist Hermann Rorschach was responsible for creating what test?

    A. IQ test
    B. Inkblot test
    C. Enneagram personality test
    D. TONI personality test

88. What did Louise Brown become famous for?

   A. Being the youngest singer to enter the Billboard charts
   B. Being the first woman in space
   C. Being the first test-tube baby
   D. Riding at the front of the bus

89. What nationality was the inventor of the first self-winding watch?

   A. French
   B. Swiss
   C. German
   D. Danish

90. In what country did the first test-tube fertilization of human eggs take place?

   A. United States
   B. Austria
   C. England
   D. Germany

91. Who was the first man in space?

   A. Yuri Gagarin
   B. Neil Armstrong
   C. Vladimir Solzchenitzyn
   D. Alan Shepard

92. What is the fastest mammal on earth?

   A. Cheetah
   B. Greyhound
   C. Leopard
   D. Horse

93. Which is not a type of shark?

    A. Whale shark
    B. Bull shark
    C. Tiger shark
    D. Grizzly shark

94. What is the speed of light?

    A. 30 million km/sec
    B. 3 million km/sec
    C. 300,000 km/sec
    D. 30,000 km/sec

95. What is the sixth planet from the sun?

    A. Jupiter
    B. Uranus
    C. Saturn
    D. Mars

96. What was the first U.S. consumer product sold in Russia?

    A. Car
    B. Soda pop
    C. Potato chips
    D. Batteries

97. What is the world's number one killer?

    A. Cancer
    B. AIDS
    C. Heart Disease
    D. Stroke

98. Who authored *Totem and Taboo*?

    A. Sigmund Freud
    B. William James
    C. Jung
    D. Watson

99. Which of the following extinct species is *not* a bird?

    A. Wake Island Rail
    B. Toolache
    C. Quelili
    D. Heath hen

100. Oology is the study of what?

    A. Insects
    B. Trees
    C. Owls
    D. Birds' eggs

101. What bone connects the shoulder blade and elbow?

    A. Humerus
    B. Scapula
    C. Ulna
    D. Carpal

102. What is the most abundant metal on earth?

    A. Pewter
    B. Iron
    C. Aluminum
    D. Brass

103. What country's satellite first photographed the far side of the moon in 1959?

    A. Russia
    B. United States
    C. Germany
    D. France

104. With what frequency does the moon orbit the earth?

    A. Every 24 days
    B. Every 24 hours
    C. Every 27 days
    D. Every 27 hours

105. Which of these inventions came first?

    A. Scotch tape
    B. Teddy bears
    C. Pocket calculator
    D. Disposable diapers

106. What percent of the Caribbean Islands are inhabited?

    A. 1%
    B. 15%
    C. 40%
    D. 60%

107. In what part of the body is insulin produced?

    A. Pancreas
    B. Pituitary gland
    C. Liver
    D. Kidney

108. What would you be ordering in a French restaurant if you selected the "fromage"?

    A. Steak
    B. Cheese
    C. Cold cuts
    D. Soup

109. Variola is the clinical name for what common infection?

    A. Measles
    B. Influenza
    C. Smallpox
    D. Chickenpox

110. What do you call the space between two adjacent neurons?

    A. Dendrite
    B. Synapse
    C. Axon
    D. Node

111. Eidology is the study of what?

    A. Rodents
    B. Ghosts
    C. Butterflies
    D. Caves

112. A quinquennium is comprised of how many years?

    A. 5
    B. 8
    C. 11
    D. 14

113. Who discovered the law of universal gravitation?

    A. Stephen Hawking
    B. Galileo Galilei
    C. Albert Einstein
    D. Sir Isaac Newton

114. What animal produces cashmere?

    A. Lamb
    B. Goat
    C. Rabbit
    D. Fox

115. How many stomachs do cows have?

    A. 1
    B. 2
    C. 3
    D. 4

116. On average, how many mink pelts are used to make a fur coat?

    A. 20
    B. 40
    C. 60
    D. 80

117. What can an oyster change during its lifetime?

    A. Setting
    B. Appearance
    C. Gender
    D. Attitude

118. On average, how long do elephants sleep per day?

    A. 2 hours
    B. 4 hours
    C. 8 hours
    D. 16 hours

119. An anencephalous creature is missing what vital organ?

    A. Heart
    B. Brain
    C. Lungs
    D. Kidney

120. A rhinologist specializes in what body part?

    A. Throat
    B. Eyes
    C. Nose
    D. Feet

CHAPTER NINE

GEOGRAPHY

1. What is the most common town name in the United States?

    A. Fairview
    B. Greenwood
    C. Springfield
    D. Oak Grove

2. What state is currently the home of the Statue of Liberty?

    A. New Jersey
    B. Rhode Island
    C. New York
    D. Connecticut

3. What city bears the nickname "The Windy City?"

    A. New York
    B. Philadelphia
    C. Chicago
    D. Boston

4. What is the only state in the U.S. that grows coffee?

    A. Texas
    B. Hawaii
    C. Illinois
    D. Wyoming

5. What is the largest U.S. city in area?

A. Los Angeles, CA
B. Chicago, IL
C. New York, NY
D. Juneau, Alaska

6. What U.S. state has the most national parks?

A. Arizona
B. Colorado
C. California
D. Alaska

7. What is the only country that is also a continent?

A. Japan
B. United Kingdom
C. Australia
D. Greenland

8. Which country's name translates in a Native American language to "Big Village"?

A. Canada
B. Morocco
C. Italy
D. Albania

9. What U.S. city has the highest murder rate, with 5.3 homicides per 100,000 people?

A. New York
B. Chicago
C. Detroit
D. Los Angeles

10. What country abolished beauty pageants in 1992?

   A. Sweden
   B. Germany
   C. Brazil
   D. Canada

11. What country is the only one to have instituted a Bill of Rights to protect cows?

   A. Pakistan
   B. Argentina
   C. India
   D. Thailand

12. What is the only great lake that does *not* extend onto Canadian territory?

   A. Lake Huron
   B. Lake Michigan
   C. Lake Erie
   D. Lake Superior

13. What country boasts more than 25% of the world's forests?

   A. Brazil
   B. Tunisia
   C. Canada
   D. Russia

14. In what nation was the highest temperature of 136 degrees recorded?

   A. Ethiopia
   B. Ecuador
   C. Libya
   D. United States

15. How much of the earth's land surface lies north of the equator?

    A. 1/8
    B. 1/4
    C. 2/3
    D. 1/2

16. What city was called the "Gateway to the West" in the 1800s?

    A. Chicago
    B. Detroit
    C. St. Louis
    D. Kansas City

17. What is the only river that flows north and south of the equator?

    A. The Congo
    B. The Thames
    C. The Volga
    D. The Nile

18. What is the largest desert, with a total land mass of over 3,565,565 square miles?

    A. Mojave
    B. Sahara
    C. Gobi
    D. Great Basin

19. What is the highest waterfall in the world?

    A. Gersoppa Falls, India
    B. Niagara Falls
    C. Angel Falls, Venezuela
    D. Kaiteur Falls, Guyana

20. In which Italian city is the Leaning Tower of Pisa located?

   A. Naples
   B. Venice
   C. Florence
   D. Pisa

21. In what country would you be if people greeted you with the phrase "Good day, mate?"

   A. England
   B. Canada
   C. United States
   D. Australia

22. What is the one state that is bordered by only one other state?

   A. Maine
   B. Hawaii
   C. Washington
   D. Alaska

23. What is the only country with a map on its flag?

   A. Peru
   B. Greece
   C. Cyprus
   D. Spain

24. What is the longest river in France?

   A. Rhone
   B. Loire
   C. Seine
   D. Danube

25. Where is the tallest building in the world, Petronas Twin Towers, located?

    A. Malaysia
    B. United States
    C. China
    D. Japan

26. What region was first to see the dawning of the new millennium?

    A. United States
    B. Canada
    C. New Zealand
    D. Antarctica

27. On what street is the White House located?

    A. Pennsylvania Avenue
    B. Washington Boulevard
    C. Constitution Avenue
    D. New York Avenue

28. Which of these is *not* of the world's oceans?

    A. Atlantic
    B. Pacific
    C. Antarctic
    D. Indian

29. What state has the longest coastline?

    A. New York
    B. Alaska
    C. Hawaii
    D. California

30. Which of the following is *not* one of the Rocky Mountain states?

    A. Idaho
    B. Montana
    C. California
    D. New Mexico

31. What state is known as the "Land of Lincoln"?

    A. Michigan
    B. Wisconsin
    C. Illinois
    D. Ohio

32. In what direction did the expedition team of Lewis and Clark travel?

    A. North
    B. South
    C. East
    D. West

33. What city was replaced by Richmond as Virginia's capital in 1779?

    A. Fredericksburg
    B. Williamsburg
    C. Alexandria
    D. Salem

34. What is the only country that has a single-color flag?

    A. Ireland
    B. Libya
    C. Israel
    D. Argentina

35. The Golden Gate Bridge is located in what city?

    A. New York
    B. Philadelphia
    C. San Francisco
    D. San Diego

36. Before it became Jerusalem, what city was Israel's capital?

    A. Tel Aviv
    B. Ovida
    C. Haifa
    D. Bethlehem

37. Which of the following has never been a Soviet Republic?

    A. Uzbekistan
    B. Kazakhstan
    C. Tajikistan
    D. Afghanistan

38. What European country is also known as "The Boot?"

    A. Germany
    B. Greece
    C. Italy
    D. Spain

39. Of the original Seven Wonders of the World, which is the only one left standing?

    A. The Pyramids of Egypt
    B. Hanging Gardens of Babylon
    C. Colossus of Rhodes
    D. Statue of Zeus at Olympia

40. What country is home to the Volcano National Park?

    A. Turkey
    B. Argentina
    C. Ecuador
    D. United States

41. Where is the source of the Mississippi River's head-waters?

    A. Minnesota
    B. Mississippi
    C. Michigan
    D. Louisiana

42. What city lies at the junction of the Allegheny and Monongahela rivers?

    A. New York
    B. Boston
    C. Philadelphia
    D. Pittsburgh

43. In what country will you find the ruins of Troy?

    A. Greece
    B. Italy
    C. Turkey
    D. Estonia

44. In what canal will you find the Pedro Miguel Lock?

    A. Suez Canal
    B. Panama Canal
    C. Erie Canal
    D. Grand Canal

45. What is Brazil's official language?

    A. Spanish
    B. Esperanto
    C. Portuguese
    D. English

46. What was the capital of West Germany?

    A. Cologne
    B. Bonn
    C. Munich
    D. Dresden

47. "The Lone Star State" is the nickname for what U.S. state?

    A. North Dakota
    B. Arizona
    C. Nevada
    D. Texas

48. What mountain range separates Asia and Europe?

    A. Appalachian mountains
    B. Ural mountains
    C. Pyrenees mountains
    D. Balkans mountains

49. Gorki Park is located in what Russian city?

    A. St. Petersburg
    B. Kazan
    C. Moscow
    D. Volgograd

50. Taipei is the capital of what nation?

    A. Singapore
    B. South Korea
    C. Japan
    D. Taiwan

51. The Hall of Mirrors is located in what French palace?

    A. The Palace of Versailles
    B. The Louvre
    C. The Hotel de Ville
    D. Notre Dame Cathedral

52. The Dead Sea is bordered by what two countries?

    A. Saudi Arabia and Israel
    B. Israel and Jordan
    C. Jordan and Turkey
    D. Iran and Saudi Arabia

53. What is the smallest of the Great Lakes?

    A. Lake Michigan
    B. Lake Erie
    C. Lake Superior
    D. Lake Ontario

54. When do most experts predict the Leaning Tower of Pisa to fall?

    A. 2000–2010
    B. 2010–2020
    C. 2020–2030
    D. 2030–2040

55. What New York street is home to "The Great White Way"?

    A. Broadway
    B. Madison Avenue
    C. Park Avenue
    D. Lexington Avenue

56. Where did the Mormons settle in 1847?

    A. New York
    B. Philadelphia
    C. Salt Lake City
    D. Minnesota

57. What is the world's smallest independent state?

    A. Liechtenstein
    B. Vatican City
    C. Monaco
    D. Luxembourg

58. What body of water separates Greece and Asia Minor?

    A. The Black Sea
    B. The Baltic Sea
    C. The Aegean Sea
    D. Mediterranean Sea

59. In what county is Chicago located?

    A. Lake County
    B. Cook County
    C. DeKalb County
    D. Cane County

60. How many U.S. states border the Pacific Ocean?

    A. 2
    B. 3
    C. 4
    D. 5

61. In what state is Myrtle Beach located?

    A. South Carolina
    B. Florida
    C. Hawaii
    D. California

62. What state is known as "The Hoosier State"?

    A. Wisconsin
    B. Illinois
    C. Indiana
    D. Michigan

63. The Mayo Clinic is located in what state?

    A. Maryland
    B. Wyoming
    C. Minnesota
    D. New York

64. What nation forms all of Hungary's northern border?

    A. Poland
    B. Bulgaria
    C. Slovakia
    D. Romania

65. What is the fifth largest country in the world?

    A. United States
    B. South Africa
    C. Japan
    D. Brazil

66. The Nile flows in what direction?

    A. North
    B. South
    C. East
    D. West

67. Where will you find the Yucatan Peninsula?

    A. Argentina
    B. Morocco
    C. Mexico
    D. Peru

68. What Italian city is home to the Trevi Fountain?

    A. Milan
    B. Venice
    C. Florence
    D. Rome

69. What is the most rural state in the United States?

    A. Vermont
    B. North Dakota
    C. Wyoming
    D. Oregon

70. What bridge spans the Hudson River?

    A. The Brooklyn Bridge
    B. The Golden Gate Bridge
    C. The George Washington Bridge
    D. The Clark Bridge

71. What country has the highest per capita consumption of cheese?

    A. Denmark
    B. France
    C. Belgium
    D. Switzerland

72. Where is the southernmost point of continental Europe?

    A. Spain
    B. France
    C. Italy
    D. Portugal

73. What is the smallest state in the United States?

    A. New Hampshire
    B. Vermont
    C. Rhode Island
    D. New Jersey

74. Which of these states does *not* border Iowa?

    A. Nebraska
    B. South Dakota
    C. Illinois
    D. Kansas

75. What is the deepest fresh-water lake in the world?

    A. Lake Baikal
    B. Lake Michigan
    C. Lake Titicaca
    D. Lake Manitoba

76. How many oceans do the United States and Canada border?

    A. One
    B. Two
    C. Three
    D. Four

77. Which is the only state allowed to fly its flag at the same height as the U.S. flag?

    A. Maryland
    B. Texas
    C. Pennsylvania
    D. New York

78. Which of the following is *not* one of the commonwealths of the United States?

    A. Massachusetts
    B. Kentucky
    C. Alabama
    D. Virginia

79. Which is the only state entirely bordered by rivers on both its east and west sides?

    A. Mississippi
    B. Idaho
    C. Illinois
    D. Iowa

80. What state is famous for being the toothpick capital of the world?

   A. Maine
   B. Delaware
   C. Nebraska
   D. Rhode Island

81. What state has the most people per square mile?

   A. New York
   B. California
   C. New Jersey
   D. Nevada

82. Which of these eastern coast states has the shortest coastline, measuring approximately fourteen miles?

   A. New Hampshire
   B. Connecticut
   C. Massachusetts
   D. Maine

83. What is the third most densely populated country in the world?

   A. The Netherlands
   B. United States
   C. China
   D. Japan

84. What do you call a person from Glasgow?

   A. Glaswegan
   B. Glaswegian
   C. Glaswenian
   D. Glaswen

85. What kind of flowers does Mt. Vernon, Washington, grow in large numbers?

    A. Daisies
    B. Carnations
    C. Sunflowers
    D. Tulips

86. From which country did the U.S. purchase Alaska?

    A. China
    B. Korea
    C. Russia
    D. England

87. What is the southernmost state in the United States?

    A. Florida
    B. Hawaii
    C. Texas
    D. Louisiana

88. Which of the following deserts does *not* fall into the cold winter desert category?

    A. Gobi
    B. Great Basin
    C. Kalahari
    D. Patagonian

89. What state is known as the "Land of 10,000 Lakes"?

    A. Wisconsin
    B. Alaska
    C. Minnesota
    D. Michigan

90. Where were the first movies made?

   A. Australia
   B. United States
   C. Germany
   D. Russia

91. Where is the Taj Mahal located?

   A. Greece
   B. Italy
   C. India
   D. Macedonia

92. What was the first country to issue postage stamps?

   A. France
   B. United States
   C. England
   D. Ireland

93. What South American country is known as "Little Venice"?

   A. Venezuela
   B. Argentina
   C. Bolivia
   D. Chile

94. What was seen in India for the first time on the big screen in 1977?

   A. Gunfight
   B. Nudity
   C. Kiss
   D. Profanity

95. On what street does the St. Patrick's Day parade travel in New York City?

A. Madison
B. Park Avenue
C. Second Avenue
D. Fifth Avenue

96. Where is the Prime Meridian located?

A. England
B. Canada
C. Spain
D. United States

97. What U.S. state is known as the "Gopher State"?

A. Maine
B. Kentucky
C. Alabama
D. Minnesota

98. In what publication was the "Pledge of Allegiance" first published?

A. *The Youth's Companion*
B. *American Heritage*
C. *LIFE*
D. *Atlantic Monthly*

99. In what state is the Alcatraz prison located?

A. Florida
B. California
C. New York
D. Rhode Island

100. How many feet deep is a fathom?

    A. 4
    B. 5
    C. 6
    D. 7

101. Who founded the American branch of the Red Cross?

    A. Abigail Adams
    B. Clara Barton
    C. Nettie Stevens
    D. Susan B. Anthony

102. What country produces the most shoes?

    A. Denmark
    B. China
    C. United States
    D. Mexico

103. What is Sweden's currency?

    A. Franc
    B. Krona
    C. Lira
    D. Peso

104. In what country would you find the Chihuahuan Desert?

    A. Canada
    B. Israel
    C. United States
    D. Saudi Arabia

105. Which of these is *not* one of the U.S. time zones?

    A. Central
    B. Pacific
    C. Eastern
    D. Western

106. What country did the Romans call Hibernia?

    A. England
    B. Greece
    C. Turkey
    D. Ireland

107. What continent has the most people per square mile?

    A. North America
    B. Asia
    C. Europe
    D. Australia

108. Which of the following is not one of the four great estuaries in England and Wales?

    A. Mersey
    B. Humber
    C. Hudson
    D. Thames

109. George Cross Island is located in what country?

    A. Malta
    B. San Marino
    C. Iceland
    D. Greece

110. Which of the following is *not* one of the three long-est rivers in the world?

    A. Nile
    B. Mississippi/Missouri
    C. Amazon
    D. Yangtze

111. Conwy, Harlech, and Beaumaris are all types of what?

    A. Bridges
    B. Cheese
    C. Trains
    D. Castles

112. What famous structure is located at Agra?

    A. Roman Colosseum
    B. Taj Mahal
    C. St. Mary's Cathedral
    D. Parthenon

113. Who is the Prime Minister of Canada?

    A. Jacques Chirac
    B. Rene Preval
    C. Jean Chretien
    D. Tony Blair

114. In what year did China become a communist state?

    A. 1941
    B. 1949
    C. 1956
    D. 1964

115. The Black Forest is located in what country?

    A. Austria
    B. France
    C. Poland
    D. Germany

116. What is the driest continent in the world?

    A. North America
    B. Antarctica
    C. Australia
    D. South America

117. What country is the world's third largest energy consumer?

    A. United States
    B. China
    C. Germany
    D. Russia

118. What is the largest lake in Australia?

    A. Lake Torrens
    B. Lake Eyre
    C. Lake Mackay
    D. Lake Gairdner

119. What country is the leading producer of gold?

    A. South Africa
    B. Australia
    C. Austria
    D. Argentina

120. What is Africa's largest country in area?

   A. Egypt
   B. Angola
   C. Sudan
   D. Libya

CHAPTER TEN

ODDS AND ENDS

1. *Serviette* is French for ...

   A. Housekeeper
   B. Tray
   C. Napkin
   D. Waiter

2. Approximately how many bricks are there in the Empire State Building?

   A. Ten thousand
   B. 100 thousand
   C. 1 million
   D. 10 million

3. How many Americans have appeared on television?

   A. 1 out of 2
   B. 1 out of 4
   C. 1 out of 10
   D. 1 out of 16

4. What zoo has the largest collection of animals?

   A. The Bronx Zoo
   B. San Diego Zoo
   C. Brookfield Zoo
   D. Los Angeles Zoo

5. What percent of the world is left-handed?

   A. 5%
   B. 10%
   C. 15%
   D. 20%

6. What does the word "karate" translate to?

   A. Closed Fist
   B. Closed Hand
   C. Open Fist
   D. Open Hand

7. What sandwich is the number one lunch choice for American kids?

   A. Bologna
   B. Grilled cheese
   C. Peanut butter and jelly
   D. Turkey

8. On what weekday do nearly 50% of bank robberies take place?

   A. Monday
   B. Wednesday
   C. Friday
   D. Sunday

9. If you bought one share of Coca-Cola in 1919, what would it be worth by 1997?

   A. $25,600
   B. $54,300
   C. $92,500
   D. $130,400

10. In 1982, Americans spent over $360 million to get rid of what?

    A. Fat
    B. Bad breath
    C. Termites
    D. Burglars

11. What was the original name for Cheerios cereal?

    A. Cheeries
    B. Cheerie bites
    C. Cheeriats
    D. Cheerioats

12. Someone who is capricious . . .

    A. Speaks well in public
    B. Socially inept
    C. Easily angered
    D. Changes their mind frequently

13. How much do Americans spend on their pets each year?

    A. $500 million
    B. $1.4 billion
    C. $5.4 billion
    D. $10.4 billion

14. According to *Food & Wine* magazine, what is Japan's favorite pizza topping?

    A. Anchovies
    B. Pepperoni
    C. Squid
    D. Mushrooms

15. Approximately how much turkey do Americans consume on Thanksgiving Day?

    A. 125 million pounds
    B. 675 million pounds
    C. 937 million pounds
    D. 1.5 billion pounds

16. What animal is *not* used to represent a year in the Chinese cycle?

    A. Boar
    B. Donkey
    C. Dragon
    D. Ox

17. What is the most popular gift among Eastern Europeans?

    A. Cigarettes
    B. Levi's jeans
    C. Vodka
    D. Caviar

18. What is the most popular fruit in America?

    A. Apples
    B. Oranges
    C. Grapes
    D. Bananas

19. What cooking term means "to slice into thin strips" in French?

    A. Flambé
    B. Frappé
    C. Chiffonade
    D. Sauté

20. SPAM is an acronym formed from which two words?

    A. Sprayed ham
    B. Spiced ham
    C. Spotted ham
    D. Spewed ham

21. What is the world's most observed holiday?

    A. New Year's Day
    B. Christmas
    C. Thanksgiving
    D. Easter

22. What do 10% of Americans leave for Santa Claus on Christmas?

    A. Mistletoe
    B. Milk and cookies
    C. Wrapped gifts
    D. Hot chocolate

23. According to Victor Borge what is the shortest distance between two people?

    A. A smile
    B. Tears
    C. Laughter
    D. Sorrow

24. How many years make up a score?

    A. 5
    B. 10
    C. 15
    D. 20

25. What is the zodiacal symbol for Aquarius?

    A. Crab
    B. Water Bearer
    C. The Twins
    D. The Virgin

26. What is the symbol for American Express on the New York Stock Exchange?

    A. Amex
    B. Amx
    C. Axp
    D. Axs

27. In England, pursuing what hobby will earn you the nickname "Twicher"?

    A. Stamp collecting
    B. Kite flying
    C. Book collecting
    D. Bird watching

28. Which of the following is *not* considered to be one of the four major hand lines in palmistry?

    A. Health
    B. Heart
    C. Life
    D. Fate

29. How many cards are there in a deck?

    A. 48
    B. 50
    C. 52
    D. 54

30. What was the original name for *Playboy* magazine?

    A. *Centerfold*
    B. *Stag Party*
    C. *Bachelor*
    D. *Bunny Hop*

31. What was the first hamburger chain in the United States?

    A. McDonald's
    B. Wendy's
    C. White Castle
    D. Hardee's

32. *Dijonnaise* is the French term for what kind of condiment?

    A. Ketchup
    B. Mustard
    C. Mayonnaise
    D. Horseradish

33. A waving white flag is an international symbol for what?

    A. Plague
    B. War
    C. Peace
    D. Death

34. Roquefort, Stilton, and Camembert are all types of what?

    A. Wines
    B. Mushrooms
    C. Flowers
    D. Cheese

35. If you're using vermouth, bourbon, bitters, and a Maraschino cherry, what drink are you mixing?

   A. Long Island Ice Tea
   B. Shirley Temple
   C. Manhattan
   D. Martini

36. Which of the following is not one of the ghosts from the video game Pac-Man?

   A. Clyde
   B. Inky
   C. Pinky
   D. Dinky

37. BVD is a type of what?

   A. Pen
   B. Underwear
   C. Watch
   D. Briefcase

38. A misanthrope is someone who hates . . .

   A. People
   B. Work
   C. Animals
   D. Flying

39. What is Bill Clinton's middle name?

   A. Samuel
   B. Jefferson
   C. Andrew
   D. Matthew

40. What is the state tree of Texas?

    A. Maple
    B. Walnut
    C. Pecan
    D. Birch

41. Before the Eiffel Tower was constructed, what building was the tallest in the world?

    A. The Roman Colosseum
    B. Notre Dame Cathedral
    C. Great Pyramid of Giza
    D. The Hermitage State Museum

42. An AK-47 assault rifle graces the flag of which country?

    A. Turkey
    B. Cuba
    C. Afghanistan
    D. Mozambique

43. What U.S. preacher was sentenced to 45 years and fined $500,000 for stealing millions from his followers?

    A. Pat Robertson
    B. Jim Bakker
    C. Rev. Rick Stevenson
    D. Jerry Falwell

44. In what language are the Dead Sea Scrolls written?

    A. Arabic
    B. Hebrew
    C. Aramaic
    D. English

45. Which of the following was *not* one of the Wise Men?

    A. Gaspar
    B. Melchior
    C. Calib
    D. Balthasar

46. Entrepreneur Ray Croc was responsible for creating what fast-food franchise?

    A. Burger King
    B. Wendy's
    C. Taco Bell
    D. McDonald's

47. BankAmericard was the original name for which credit card?

    A. Master Card
    B. Discover
    C. Visa
    D. American Express

48. What organization boasts the motto "Be prepared"?

    A. Girl Scouts
    B. American Red Cross
    C. Save the Children
    D. Boy Scouts

49. What car manufacturer introduced the Edsel, one of the world's worst-selling cars?

    A. Chrysler
    B. General Motors
    C. Ford
    D. Dodge

50. Ancient Egyptians worshiped which animals, building pyramids for their burials?

   A. Cows
   B. Cats
   C. Dogs
   D. Rabbits

51. What Mafioso was known as "The Teflon Don"?

   A. Al Capone
   B. Paul Castellano
   C. John Gotti
   D. Aniello "Neil" Dellacroce

52. What did Benjamin "Bugsy" Siegel name his first Las Vegas casino?

   A. Caesar's Palace
   B. Lady Luck
   C. Tropicana
   D. The Flamingo

53. What is the oldest college in the United States?

   A. Yale
   B. Harvard
   C. Princeton
   D. William and Mary

54. Who was *Time* magazine's person of the year in 1999?

   A. Jeff Bezos
   B. Hillary Clinton
   C. Madeline Albright
   D. Sumner Redstone

55. What sea parted for Moses as he led the Jews out
of Egypt?

A. The Dead Sea
B. The Black Sea
C. The Red Sea
D. The Yellow Sea

56. John D. Rockefeller made his first fortune in which
business?

A. Publishing
B. Engineering
C. Oil
D. Pharmaceuticals

57. What woman has appeared on the most covers of
Time magazine?

A. Margaret Thatcher
B. Mother Theresa
C. Princess Diana
D. The Virgin Mary

58. What was the world's first speed-limit law, enacted
in England in 1903?

A. 10 mph
B. 20 mph
C. 30 mph
D. 40 mph

59. Which of these is *not* one of the Bible's seven
deadly sins?

A. Avarice
B. Greed
C. Sloth
D. Pride

60. Which of these women has *not* been represented on U.S. currency?

 A. Martha Washington
 B. Pocahontas
 C. Susan B. Anthony
 D. Amelia Earhart

61. Four thousand years ago in Egypt, what was the penalty for killing a cat?

 A. Caning
 B. Jail
 C. Severing a limb
 D. Death

62. In the Bible, what did Jacob change his name to?

 A. Moses
 B. Israel
 C. Ishmael
 D. Noah

63. What was Dr. Watson's first name?

 A. David
 B. Thomas
 C. Richard
 D. John

64. The Harley-Davidson Co. manufactures what kind of product?

 A. Sports gear
 B. Motorcycles
 C. Tires
 D. Lighting

65. Who became the first billionaire in 1916?

    A. Andrew Carnegie
    B. John D. Rockefeller
    C. Aristotle Onassis
    D. John Paul Getty

66. What New York newspaper first published Robert
    Ripley's strip "Believe it or Not"?

    A. *New York Times*
    B. *New York Post*
    C. *New York Inquirer*
    D. *New York Globe*

67. How much did the first trans-Atlantic phone call
    cost for a three-minute conversation?

    A. $75
    B. $100
    C. $125
    D. $150

68. What solvent removes paint stains?

    A. Turpentine
    B. Alcohol
    C. Ginger ale
    D. Vick's VaporRub

69. Who founded the Mormons or Latter-day Saints in
    New York?

    A. Joseph Smith
    B. John D. Lee
    C. Wilford Woodruff
    D. George Cannon

70. What was the first department store opened in America in 1877?

   A. Bloomingdale's
   B. Macy's
   C. Wanamaker's
   D. Lord & Taylor

71. What television network used a peacock for its logo?

   A. NBC
   B. CBS
   C. ABC
   D. WB

72. Which of the following is *not* one of the new TV ratings codes implemented in 1997?

   A. TV-Y
   B. TV-G
   C. TV-PG
   D. TV-R

73. Before changing its name to Columbia University, what was the learning institution in New York known as?

   A. New York College
   B. Kings College
   C. Freedom University
   D. Manhattan College

74. Which of the following is David Letterman's alma mater?

    A. Tulane University
    B. Colgate University
    C. Ball State University
    D. The University of Indiana

75. Which of the following poker hands is the highest?

    A. Flush
    B. Three of a kind
    C. Straight
    D. Two pair

76. Which of the following candies was named after a race horse?

    A. Breathmint
    B. Lollypop
    C. Toffee
    D. Jelly bean

77. What is the longest day of the year?

    A. The autumn equinox
    B. The winter solstice
    C. The summer solstice
    D. The spring equinox

78. According to the Old Testament, whose wife turned into a pillar of salt?

    A. Noah's
    B. Able's
    C. Joseph's
    D. Lot's

79. What kind of number is 7?

   A. Round
   B. Prime
   C. Even
   D. Negative

80. Which of the following is a fruit?

   A. Corn
   B. Tomato
   C. Lettuce
   D. Carrot

81. Queen Esther plays a crucial role in what Jewish holiday?

   A. Hanukkah
   B. Sukkoth
   C. Passover
   D. Purim

82. According to legend, what did the first man to ever run a marathon meet with at the end of his trek?

   A. Death
   B. Capture and imprisonment
   C. Partial paralysis
   D. Swamp land

83. Which religion professes that Christ cast Satan out of Heaven in 1914?

   A. The Latter-Day Saints
   B. Jehovah's Witnesses
   C. Christian Science
   D. Islam

84. Which is not one of the four "C"s used to evaluate the value of a diamond?

    A. Color
    B. Cut
    C. Clarity
    D. Curve

85. Which of the following is *not* a type of Barbie doll?

    A. Birthday Barbie
    B. Perfect Hair Barbie
    C. Western Barbie
    D. Beauty Secrets Barbie

86. What city is the site of the U.S.A.'s first pizzeria?

    A. Chicago
    B. San Francisco
    C. New York
    D. Pittsburgh

87. What decade saw the invention of the bread slicing machine?

    A. 1910s
    B. 1920s
    C. 1930s
    D. 1940s

88. What was the name given to the first person to be recognized as a major transmitter of AIDS?

    A. Agent of Death
    B. Patient Zero
    C. Carrier One
    D. First Contact

89. What product was not introduced to the U.S. by Wham-O?

    A. The slingshot
    B. The Frisbee
    C. The Hula-Hoop
    D. The Hackensack Ball

90. What game manufacturer's name translates to "work hard, but in the end, it is in Heaven's hands"?

    A. Atari
    B. Nintendo
    C. Sega
    D. Tetris

91. What fruit has the highest amount of Vitamin C?

    A. Orange
    B. Banana
    C. Strawberry
    D. Apple

92. What is the waiting period to purchase a gun in Colorado?

    A. 0 days
    B. 1 days
    C. 2 days
    D. 1 week

93. Who was the first celebrity on the cover of *People* magazine?

    A. Warren Beatty
    B. Farrah Fawcett
    C. Mia Farrow
    D. Tom Selleck

94. On average, how many wisdom teeth does an adult have?

    A. Five
    B. Four
    C. Three
    D. Two

95. A colander is used for what culinary purpose?

    A. Draining pasta
    B. Dicing onions
    C. Decorating cakes
    D. Mashing potatoes

96. What is the character's name on the Frosted Flakes cereal box?

    A. Lenny the Lion
    B. Tony the Tiger
    C. Chucky the Chimp
    D. Barney the Dinosaur

97. A group of kittens is called a . . .

    A. Sleuth
    B. Kindle
    C. Caboodle
    D. Bundle

98. What name is given to the final round on the game *The Price is Right*?

    A. Play off
    B. Finals
    C. Showdown
    D. Showcase

99. A roulette wheel is comprised of how many compartments?

   A. 37
   B. 42
   C. 46
   D. 49

100. Mountaineers are guided by what patron saint?

   A. St. Bernard
   B. St. Francis
   C. St. Christopher
   D. St. Adela

101. In the *Wizard of Oz*, what did Dorothy have to steal from the Wicked Witch of the West?

   A. Red shoes
   B. Umbrella
   C. Broom
   D. Crystal ball

102. The Rubik's Cube was introduced in what year?

   A. 1975
   B. 1979
   C. 1983
   D. 1986

103. Approximately how much does the human liver weigh?

   A. 1 lbs.
   B. 3 lbs.
   C. 6 lbs
   D. 9 lbs.

104. What is the term for a group of dolphins?

    A. Squall
    B. Clump
    C. School
    D. Pod

105. What item of clothing was first designed for actress Jane Russell?

    A. Garter belt
    B. Women's pants
    C. Brassiere
    D. Knickers

106. What car manufacturer bought out Rolls-Royce in 1998?

    A. Volkswagen
    B. Mercedes
    C. Ford
    D. BMW

107. The Murano district is popular for producing what product?

    A. Glass
    B. Wine
    C. Silk
    D. Cheese

108. The Rialto bridge is located in what Italian city?

    A. Florence
    B. Rome
    C. Milan
    D. Venice

109. What is the name of Popeye's son?

   A. Sweet Pea
   B. Popeye Junior
   C. Paulie
   D. Simon

110. Who replaced Jenny McCarthy as cohost of MTV's dating show *Singled Out*?

   A. LaToya Jackson
   B. Pamela Anderson
   C. Carmen Electra
   D. Jennifer Lopez

111. In what state will you find the Ben & Jerry ice cream factory?

   A. Wyoming
   B. Maryland
   C. Vermont
   D. Michigan

112. What U.S. government agency is also known as "The Brotherhood"?

   A. CIA
   B. FCC
   C. FBI
   D. IRS

113. Which of the following is *not* a term for a real region?

   A. Sun Belt
   B. Bible Belt
   C. Grain Belt
   D. Borscht Belt

114. The Hawaiian alphabet has how many letters?

    A. 12
    B. 24
    C. 38
    D. 50

115. What game utilizes a total of five dice?

    A. Monopoly
    B. Scattegories
    C. Backgammon
    D. Yahtzee

116. What family members won a total of five Grammy Awards in 1998?

    A. Julio and Enrique Iglesias
    B. Bob and Jakob Dylan
    C. Janet and Michael Jackson
    D. The Hansons

117. Janet Jackson has what cartoon character tattooed on her body?

    A. Donald Duck
    B. Jerry the mouse
    C. The Road Runner
    D. Micky Mouse

118. Which of these quiz shows was first to air?

    A. *Who Wants to be a Millionaire*
    B. *The $64,000 Question*
    C. *Twenty-One*
    D. *Jeopardy*

119. What country is the world's leading exporter of sugar?

    A. Jamaica
    B. Cuba
    C. Brazil
    D. United States

120. What was rated the most claustrophobic job in the U.S.?

    A. Pilot
    B. Telephone booth repairman
    C. Elevator operator
    D. Astronaut

ANSWERS TO TRIVIA QUESTIONS

CHAPTER FOUR—ENTERTAINMENT

1. C	28. D	55. D
2. A	29. A	56. C
3. D	30. C	57. D
4. C	31. B	58. A
5. B	32. B	59. C
6. B	33. B	60. B
7. C	34. C	61. B
8. C	35. A	62. B
9. D	36. B	63. C
10. D	37. C	64. B
11. B	38. D	65. A
12. B	39. A	66. B
13. C	40. D	67. B
14. B	41. A	68. A
15. A	42. B	69. D
16. C	43. C	70. B
17. A	44. D	71. A
18. C	45. A	72. B
19. B	46. C	73. C
20. D	47. D	74. C
21. A	48. A	75. B
22. B	49. A	76. A
23. D	50. B	77. B
24. B	51. D	78. C
25. D	52. B	79. A
26. A	53. C	80. C
27. D	54. B	81. C

82. D	95. D	108. C
83. C	96. A	109. C
84. B	97. A	110. B
85. C	98. B	111. A
86. A	99. D	112. C
87. B	100. C	113. C
88. D	101. B	114. C
89. D	102. D	115. A
90. B	103. C	116. B
91. D	104. D	117. B
92. A	105. C	118. B
93. B	106. D	119. A
94. B	107. B	120. B

CHAPTER FIVE—HISTORY AND POLITICS

1. C	23. D	45. B
2. A	24. A	46. A
3. B	25. B	47. B
4. B	26. C	48. B
5. C	27. C	49. A
6. B	28. A	50. C
7. A	29. B	51. D
8. D	30. A	52. C
9. C	31. C	53. B
10. B	32. A	54. C
11. D	33. D	55. A
12. A	34. B	56. B
13. B	35. D	57. C
14. C	36. C	58. B
15. A	37. C	59. B
16. C	38. D	60. C
17. C	39. C	61. A
18. A	40. A	62. C
19. A	41. A	63. B
20. D	42. B	64. A
21. D	43. B	65. B
22. B	44. C	66. D

67. A	85. C	103. A
68. C	86. A	104. B
69. B	87. C	105. B
70. D	88. C	106. A
71. B	89. B	107. B
72. C	90. B	108. C
73. B	91. A	109. B
74. B	92. B	110. A
75. D	93. B	111. C
76. B	94. D	112. D
77. C	95. B	113. B
78. A	96. C	114. C
79. B	97. B	115. D
80. C	98. A	116. D
81. A	99. C	117. B
82. C	100. D	118. B
83. D	101. C	119. C
84. A	102. C	120. C

CHAPTER SIX—ART AND LITERATURE

1. C	18. D	35. D
2. C	19. C	36. D
3. C	20. C	37. A
4. A	21. A	38. C
5. A	22. C	39. C
6. C	23. D	40. D
7. A	24. C	41. B
8. A	25. A	42. A
9. C	26. B	43. A
10. C	27. B	44. B
11. C	28. D	45. D
12. A	29. B	46. D
13. C	30. C	47. B
14. D	31. D	48. D
15. D	32. B	49. D
16. A	33. D	50. B
17. B	34. B	51. C

52. B	75. C	98. B
53. A	76. A	99. A
54. C	77. B	100. C
55. D	78. C	101. B
56. B	79. C	102. C
57. D	80. A	103. B
58. B	81. A	104. B
59. C	82. B	105. C
60. D	83. C	106. A
61. B	84. D	107. C
62. A	85. C	108. B
63. A	86. B	109. A
64. B	87. C	110. A
65. C	88. B	111. C
66. D	89. C	112. B
67. C	90. B	113. C
68. B	91. B	114. A
69. D	92. C	115. A
70. D	93. D	116. C
71. B	94. D	117. D
72. A	95. B	118. A
73. A	96. B	119. B
74. A	97. C	120. B

CHAPTER SEVEN—SPORTS

1. B	13. C	25. D
2. A	14. D	26. C
3. A	15. C	27. D
4. B	16. B	28. A
5. A	17. D	29. B
6. C	18. C	30. C
7. B	19. B	31. B
8. C	20. A	32. D
9. B	21. C	33. B
10. D	22. A	34. C
11. C	23. D	35. D
12. B	24. B	36. D

37. A	65. C	93. B
38. A	66. B	94. D
39. B	67. B	95. B
40. C	68. D	96. B
41. A	69. D	97. C
42. C	70. C	98. C
43. B	71. A	99. A
44. B	72. B	100. C
45. B	73. D	101. B
46. A	74. C	102. C
47. B	75. D	103. C
48. A	76. C	104. C
49. C	77. A	105. B
50. B	78. A	106. C
51. D	79. B	107. B
52. B	80. D	108. C
53. A	81. C	109. A
54. C	82. A	110. B
55. C	83. A	111. D
56. A	84. B	112. B
57. B	85. C	113. B
58. C	86. A	114. A
59. D	87. A	115. C
60. A	88. A	116. B
61. C	89. A	117. C
62. B	90. B	118. B
63. A	91. A	119. D
64. A	92. B	120. D

CHAPTER EIGHT—SCIENCE AND TECHNOLOGY

1. C	7. D	13. B
2. A	8. B	14. B
3. C	9. C	15. A
4. C	10. C	16. B
5. C	11. A	17. C
6. C	12. C	18. C

19. A	53. A	87. B
20. C	54. D	88. C
21. C	55. B	89. B
22. B	56. D	90. C
23. C	57. A	91. A
24. A	58. B	92. A
25. B	59. C	93. D
26. D	60. C	94. C
27. B	61. D	95. C
28. A	62. B	96. B
29. D	63. B	97. C
30. C	64. D	98. A
31. B	65. C	99. B
32. A	66. A	100. D
33. D	67. B	101. A
34. B	68. C	102. C
35. A	69. C	103. A
36. B	70. B	104. C
37. C	71. A	105. B
38. B	72. C	106. A
39. C	73. B	107. A
40. D	74. C	108. B
41. C	75. B	109. C
42. D	76. A	110. B
43. C	77. A	111. B
44. D	78. D	112. A
45. C	79. A	113. D
46. A	80. B	114. B
47. B	81. A	115. D
48. C	82. D	116. C
49. A	83. B	117. C
50. D	84. B	118. A
51. A	85. A	119. B
52. B	86. B	120. C

CHAPTER NINE—GEOGRAPHY

1. A	36. A	71. B
2. A	37. D	72. A
3. C	38. C	73. C
4. B	39. A	74. D
5. D	40. D	75. A
6. D	41. A	76. C
7. C	42. D	77. B
8. A	43. C	78. C
9. C	44. B	79. D
10. D	45. C	80. A
11. C	46. B	81. C
12. B	47. D	82. A
13. D	48. B	83. D
14. C	49. C	84. B
15. C	50. D	85. D
16. C	51. A	86. C
17. A	52. B	87. B
18. B	53. D	88. C
19. C	54. B	89. C
20. D	55. A	90. B
21. D	56. C	91. C
22. A	57. B	92. C
23. C	58. C	93. A
24. B	59. B	94. C
25. A	60. D	95. D
26. C	61. A	96. A
27. A	62. C	97. D
28. C	63. C	98. A
29. B	64. C	99. B
30. C	65. D	100. A
31. C	66. A	101. B
32. D	67. C	102. B
33. B	68. D	103. B
34. B	69. B	104. C
35. C	70. C	105. D

106. D	111. D	116. B
107. C	112. B	117. D
108. C	113. C	118. B
109. A	114. B	119. A
110. D	115. D	120. C

CHAPTER TEN—ODDS AND ENDS

1. C	31. C	61. D
2. D	32. B	62. B
3. B	33. C	63. D
4. B	34. D	64. B
5. B	35. C	65. B
6. D	36. D	66. D
7. C	37. B	67. A
8. C	38. A	68. A
9. C	39. B	69. A
10. B	40. C	70. C
11. D	41. C	71. A
12. D	42. D	72. D
13. C	43. B	73. B
14. C	44. C	74. C
15. B	45. C	75. A
16. B	46. D	76. B
17. C	47. C	77. C
18. D	48. D	78. D
19. C	49. C	79. B
20. B	50. B	80. B
21. A	51. C	81. D
22. B	52. D	82. A
23. C	53. B	83. B
24. D	54. A	84. D
25. B	55. C	85. B
26. C	56. C	86. C
27. D	57. D	87. B
28. A	58. B	88. B
29. C	59. B	89. D
30. B	60. D	90. B

91. C	101. C	111. C
92. A	102. B	112. A
93. C	103. B	113. C
94. B	104. D	114. A
95. A	105. C	115. D
96. B	106. A	116. B
97. B	107. A	117. D
98. D	108. D	118. B
99. A	109. A	119. B
100. A	110. C	120. D

AUTHORS' BIO

Elina and Leah Furman live and write in New York City. When they're not obsessing about making millions on quiz shows, they spend their time writing numerous entertainment biographies and self-help books.

GET ALL THE COOL FACTS ON YOUR FAVORITE CELEBS!

MATT DAMON
0-312-96857-4___$4.99___$6.50 Can.

SALMA HAYEK
0-312-96982-1___$4.99___$6.50 Can.

JENNIFER LOPEZ
0-312-97085-4___$4.99___$6.50 Can.

JENNIFER LOVE HEWITT
0-312-96991-0___$4.99___$6.50 Can.

EWAN McGREGOR
0-312-96910-4___$5.99___$7.99 Can.

WILL SMITH
0-312-96722-5___$4.99___$6.50 Can.

JAMES VAN DER BEEK
0-312-97226-1___$5.99___$7.99 Can.